Accessing the Curriculum f
with Autism Spectrum Disc

This brand new edition of *Accessing the Curriculum for Learners with Autism Spectrum Disorders* will provide educators with the principles and practices of Structured Teaching and how to apply these to enable learners to access the curriculum, whatever that curriculum may be.

This unique resource is intended to be essential reading for schools and settings who are keen to implement Structured Teaching as an approach to including learners on the autism spectrum in teaching and learning. With a wide range of helpful advice and support, this book:

- demonstrates how to make use of the approach to address diverse needs, overcome barriers to learning and achieve successful differentiation;
- uses case studies and examples that illustrate how the approach is applicable across Early Years, Primary, Secondary and vocational curricula;
- provides the physical structure, schedules, work systems and visual information necessary to illustrate use of these components to promote curriculum access, with an emphasis on understanding and meaning.

This new edition is fully updated to include examples of new technologies and is suitable for use in a range of international educational contexts. It also includes a brand new chapter on blending Structured Teaching with other approaches.

Gary Mesibov is a distinguished psychologist and professor emeritus at the University of North Carolina and is former director of Division TEACCH. Professor Mesibov continues to lecture, train, teach and mentor worldwide.

Marie Howley is a senior lecturer in SEN and Inclusion (Autism) in the School of Education at the University of Northampton and has experience as a TEACCH trainer in the UK and North Carolina.

Signe Naftel works as an adjunct professor at the TEACCH program in Chapel Hill, North Carolina.

Accessing the Curriculum for Learners with Autism Spectrum Disorders

Using the TEACCH programme to help inclusion

2nd edition

Gary Mesibov and Marie Howley
with Signe Naftel

Routledge
Taylor & Francis Group

LONDON AND NEW YORK

Second edition published 2016
by Routledge
2 Park Square, Milton Park, Abingdon, Oxon OX14 4RN

and by Routledge
711 Third Avenue, New York, NY 10017

Routledge is an imprint of the Taylor & Francis Group, an informa business

© 2016 G. Mesibov, M. Howley and S. Naftel

First published 2003 by David Fulton Publishers

British Library Cataloguing-in-Publication Data
A catalogue record for this book is available from the British Library

Library of Congress Cataloging in Publication Data
Mesibov, Gary B.
Accessing the curriculum for learners with autism spectrum disorders : using the TEACCH programme to help inclusion / Gary Mesibov and Marie Howley. – Second edition.
  pages cm
  Includes bibliographical references and index.
  1. Autistic children–Education–Great Britain. 2. Inclusive education–Great Britain. 3. Mainstreaming in education–Great Britain. I. Howley, Marie. II. Title.
  LC4718.5.G7M47 2016
  371.9–dc23   2015005343

ISBN: 978-0-415-72819-5 (hbk)
ISBN: 978-0-415-72820-1 (pbk)
ISBN: 978-1-315-68378-2 (ebk)

Typeset in Sabon
by Wearset Ltd, Boldon, Tyne and Wear
Printed in Great Britain by Ashford Colour Press Ltd

Dedicated to Terry Arnold who did so much to improve the lives of people with autism in the world and especially in playing a pivotal role in bringing the TEACCH ideas to the UK.

Contents

Figures

Tables

Preface

As with the first edition of this book, this second edition was inspired by many professionals who are using Division TEACCH's Structured Teaching as part of their autism-friendly good practice. Again, as with the first edition, this is not a manual about Division TEACCH, nor how to implement Structured Teaching. Instead, it represents our efforts to show how Structured Teaching can be used to advance educational goals and priorities for learners on the autism spectrum. The first edition focused upon how Structured Teaching can be used to enable learners to access the UK National Curriculum, due to requests from those who were being asked to justify their use of the approach. Since that time, it has become clear that the *principles* illustrated in the case studies of the first edition are equally applicable across a variety of different curricula and are not unique to any particular curriculum. In addition, Structured Teaching has continued to spread around the world as practitioners and families have discovered the importance of structure in the lives of individuals with autism.

This new edition of our book therefore includes three additional case studies in each chapter which represent examples of using Structured Teaching in North Carolina, USA, Denmark and India. These additional case studies demonstrate that Structured Teaching is an effective strategy to enable learners to access a curriculum, whatever that curriculum may be. The new case studies illustrate developments in using Structured Teaching and include examples of using new technologies to present structure. In addition, one of the case studies includes older learners who are able to use Structured Teaching to access a vocational curriculum. Each of the case studies is presented in Chapters 4–7, illustrating how physical structure, schedules, work systems and visual information can be implemented to enhance curriculum access and meaningful learning.

In addition to the new case studies, we have included a final new chapter which considers how Structured Teaching may be combined with other educational approaches, thus reflecting the real-world eclectic approach to educating children and young people with autism spectrum disorders. This chapter illustrates how Structured Teaching provides a framework within which other approaches can be implemented according to individual needs.

Throughout this book we have used the term autism spectrum disorders (ASD) to describe our population of learners, ranging from those who have additional severe learning disabilities to those with average to above average academic ability. This terminology corresponds to our view of autism as more than a single, finite developmental disability, but rather a continuum of difficulties, ranging from mild to severe, involving social problems, communication difficulties and restricted and repetitive behaviours, activities and interests. The book also reflects the strengths and special interests that are integral to making Structured Teaching as effective as possible. We have taken the editorial prerogative of using the term 'he' to refer to our population. This was chosen because of the higher ratio of males to females that is found throughout the autism literature.

We sincerely hope that this second edition of our book will be of help to our many friends, colleagues, families and other interested citizens who have expressed an interest in this subject.

Acknowledgements

As with the first edition, this book would not have been completed without the help of many dedicated people. We are enormously grateful to the contributors who gave up their valuable time, and sometimes their classrooms, to provide examples and illustrations of their professional practice. Special thanks go to Mansi Bagwe, Kathy Hearsey and Susanne Hvidtfeldt who were so generous with their time and so patient with us as we developed the new case studies which feature in each chapter.

Finally a special thank you to the children and young people and their families who make sure that we know when the structure is working.

Contributors to case studies

Mansi Bagwe, MA (Edu) UK, Director, Care4Autism Centre & Autism Friendly School, Telangana, India
Kathy Hearsey, MEd Assistant Director of Training, TEACCH Autism Program, North Carolina, USA
Susanne Hvidtfeldt, educated as a teacher and worked in the autism field since 1985, and is a consultant at Langagerskolen special school, Aarhus, Denmark
Green Oaks Lower School, Designated Special Provision (DSP): Northamptonshire
Kingsley Special School: Northamptonshire
Kingsthorpe Grove Lower School, DSP: Northamptonshire
Linden Bridge School: Surrey
Peak School: Derbyshire
Radlett Lodge, The National Autistic Society: Hertfordshire
Rowan Gate Primary School: Northamptonshire
Samuel Whitbread Community College: Bedfordshire
Special Educational Needs and Psychology Service: Essex
Sunfield School: Worcestershire

Chapter 1

Overview of the autism spectrum

Autism spectrum disorders

The word 'autism' first appeared in the professional literature when Leo Kanner, a child psychiatrist at Johns Hopkins University in Baltimore, MD, wrote a description of 11 children from his child psychiatric unit in 1943. These children were different from the others in his unit who were diagnosed with Childhood Schizophrenia. The children Kanner wrote about in his original paper had little interest in other people, peculiar language, an insistence on routines, and they displayed unusual body movements and repetitive behaviours.

Kanner's original description emphasised three areas of difficulty: social isolation, abnormal communication and an insistence on repetitive, narrow routines. These major areas of impairment have continued to be the foundation of the autism diagnosis in the major diagnostic systems used throughout the world.

The definition of autism spectrum disorders has transformed over the years, but the 'triad of impairments' (Wing and Gould 1979) has remained central to the diagnosis of autism. The most recent transformation of the definition of ASD occurred in 2013 when the term Pervasive Developmental Disorders (PDD) shifted to the umbrella term Autism Spectrum Disorder (ASD) in the DSM-5 (American Psychiatric Association 2013). Current diagnostic systems, DSM-5 and ICD-10 (WHO 1992), define ASD as differences in social communication and social interaction skills as well as restricted behaviours or interests. Communication differences are not considered a separate diagnostic criterion, as is in previous definitions, but instead, are thought to be intertwined with social impairments. Therefore, communication differences are contextualised within the social communication and social interaction diagnostic criterion. In order to qualify for the ASD diagnosis, a person must demonstrate deficits in the areas of social communication and interaction as well as repetitive behaviours or interests.

ASD is a broad continuum of functioning levels, with similar core characteristics of social communication difficulties and repetitive behaviours/interests. Specific characteristics within the social communication and social interaction criterion include deficits in social-emotional reciprocity, deficits in non-verbal communication, and deficits in social relationships. Specific characteristics in the restricted, repetitive patterns of behaviour/interests include stereotyped motor movements, inflexibility, highly restricted interests, or unusual sensory differences. Not all characteristics are required for a diagnosis, but characteristics are required to be present in the early developmental periods. Additionally, severity level along the continuum must be specified. Severity levels for ASD are categorised as Level 1 'Requiring support', Level 2 'Requiring some support' and Level 3 'Requiring very substantial support' (DSM-5).

Prior to this current definition of ASD, the term Pervasive Developmental Disorders (PDD) was used as the umbrella category of all people showing impairments or peculiarities in these three areas, including more subtle ones. Various diagnoses existed within the PDD category, autism being the best-known and most widely used diagnostic category within the autism spectrum. Autism was defined as differences in three areas: communication, socialisation and repetitive behaviour, which is similar to the current definition, but with communication being a separate category. In addition to autism, several other specific diagnostic classifications were considered distinguishable from classical autism because of their characteristics, including Pervasive Developmental Disorder – Not Otherwise Specified (PPD-NOS), Asperger Syndrome, Rett's Syndrome, and Childhood Disintegrative Disorder.

PDD-NOS referred to those people on the autism spectrum who share many of the characteristics, but might not show the precise number of characteristics required for the autism diagnosis, or they might not have the marked deficits or peculiarities in the social area that are necessary. Many professionals viewed PDD-NOS (Atypical Autism) as a milder form of autism. Another diagnosis that fell within the autism spectrum in the previous conceptualisation was Asperger Syndrome (AS). The definition of AS was similar to autism, but the primary difference was in the area of communication; a person did not have to demonstrate any communication difficulties to qualify for the AS diagnosis. In fact, it was a requirement that their language developed at the normal time, using words by the age of two and simple phrases by age three. For a diagnosis of AS, it was also required that a person have an average or above average IQ.

Finally, two other less common diagnoses were included in earlier conceptualisations of the PDD umbrella. These diagnoses are Rett's Syndrome and Childhood Disintegrative Disorder. PDD-NOS, AS, Rett's Syndrome and Childhood Disintegrative Disorder no longer formally exist under the new umbrella of ASD, though Rett's Syndrome is mentioned as a neuro-genetic disorder. Individuals with a previous diagnosis of AS and PDD-NOS should instead be considered as having ASD. This conceptualisation is considered simpler, as it is one continuum rather than several separate diagnoses.

To summarise, ASD is a continuum of characteristics, with a wide range of severity. While some individuals with ASD are non-verbal, others are highly verbal, but have difficulty using their language for social reasons. The commonality across the spectrum is difficulty with social communication, social interaction, and displaying repetitive, restricted interests or behaviours.

Overlapping disorders

It is a major challenge identifying people with ASDs and determining where they appear on the continuum. It is also difficult to distinguish ASDs from related conditions because there are sometimes significant areas of overlap. Diagnoses with the greatest overlap that are most frequently confused with ASDs are Obsessive-Compulsive Disorder (OCD), Social (pragmatic) Communication Disorder, Attention Deficit Hyperactivity Disorder (ADHD) and Schizoid Personality Disorder.

Obsessive-Compulsive Disorder is identified by repetitive thoughts and/or behaviours. A distinction is usually made between obsessions, which are recurrent and persistent thoughts, and compulsions, which are non-functional repetitive behaviours. Sometimes the distinctions between OCD and ASDs are difficult to distinguish because many people with ASDs have repetitive thoughts or behaviours. Some differences that help professionals make these discriminations are that most people with OCD are secretive about their repetitive ideas or behaviours because they realise that other people would consider them bizarre. Those affected with OCD usually wish that the routines would go away and feel great anxiety when thinking about or performing them. This is very different from people with ASDs, who have little insight into the non-productive nature of their repetitive behaviours or how these behaviours impact on others. Often people with ASD feel calm, engaged, and even joyful when thinking about and performing their rituals, rather than anxious.

It is important for clinicians to understand that the narrow interests associated with ASDs are not the same as obsessive thoughts. The preoccupations that these youngsters think and talk about are much less likely to be the sex, religion or bodily concerns that are more frequently seen in OCD. Developmental histories can also be helpful in making these distinctions. People with OCD usually do not have preschool or early onset of these preoccupations and other developmental difficulties. The earlier onset of these obsessions or compulsions, plus other developmental problems, are much more typical in ASDs.

Social (pragmatic) Communication Disorder (SCD) is a developmental language disorder characterised by problems in the social use of verbal and non-verbal communication (DSM-5, 2013). People who fall within this diagnostic classification show several similarities to ASDs. They have problems with some of the same aspects of interpersonal communication, including difficulties initiating and sustaining conversations, staying on topics, matching their communication style to the context, and understanding subtleties. The primary difference from ASD is that people with social communication disorder do not display repetitive or stereotyped behaviours/interests, as do people with ASD.

Another diagnostic category that overlaps with ASD is Attention Deficit Hyperactivity Disorder (ADHD). ADHD is used to describe people who have difficulty paying attention and controlling their behaviour and activity levels. People in this group can often resemble people with ASD because they appear not to listen when addressed, they have difficulty following verbal directions, problems with concentration, a reluctance to engage in certain tasks, problems with impulse control, and excessive talking.

Even though there are many similarities between ADHD and ASD, the underlying reasons for the difficulties are usually different. For children with ADHD, there appears to be a neurological problem limiting their focused attention that can have implications for social and communication difficulties. It is not that these children can't understand language or social nuances, it is rather that they have difficulty focusing and maintaining their attention in appropriate ways at appropriate times. For people with ASD, their problem is not necessarily limited attention but rather a different way of focusing their attention. It has been suggested that their focus is more narrow and intense and that they also have difficulty shifting their attention. Social and communication difficulties for people with ASD are usually the reasons why they have problems communicating and also with understanding and responding to directions. It is these social and communication problems that make interaction difficult, in addition to their attentional differences, rather than simply their attentional problems.

A final condition that is sometimes confused with ASD is Schizoid Personality Disorder. This disorder is characterised by a 'pervasive pattern of detachment from social relationships and a restricted range of expression of emotions in interpersonal settings' (DSM-5, American Psychiatric Association 2013: 652). Problems with social skills and friendship, aloofness, an apparent insensitivity to others and a narrow single-mindedness are characteristics that this group shares with people with ASD. The differences, however, are that people with Schizoid Personality Disorder have less severe problems with interpersonal relationships, and they manifest themselves later in the school years or in early adulthood, rather than in the preschool and early school years, as is seen with ASD. Communication problems among individuals with Schizoid Personality are also more limited. These individuals show a capacity for imagination and fantasy, and they do not have the narrow special interests of people with ASD. There also seems to be a genetic link between Schizoid Personality Disorder and other psychiatric conditions.

In spite of these differences, Wolff (1998) argues that Schizoid Personality Disorder might be part of the autism spectrum. She argues that many of the effective intervention approaches used with higher functioning people with ASD can also be used effectively with this group, even though they are slightly more socially skilled, independent, and have a better long-term prognosis.

Summary

In summary, those who receive a diagnosis of ASD have many important similarities to one another, especially in the areas of social interaction, social communication, perseveration and conceptualisation. These common characteristics have important implications for educational programmes and provision and will be the major focus of this book. Learners with overlapping, but different, diagnoses will share enough common characteristics that they will probably benefit from some of the educational strategies described in the chapters that follow.

Chapter 2

Structured Teaching as a foundation for educational programmes

Division TEACCH

Division TEACCH (Treatment and Education of Autistic and related Communication handicapped Children) is North Carolina's statewide programme serving people with ASD and their families. The programme was initially funded by the Federal Government in 1966. At that point, ASD was viewed as an emotional disorder and parents were seen as the main cause. Terms like 'refrigerator mother' were commonly used to describe these parents and convey how cold, aloof and sometimes rejecting behaviours might cause ASD in their children.

Eric Schopler, co-founder and the first director of Division TEACCH, was among the pioneers in establishing ASD as a developmental disorder and demonstrating that parents did not cause ASD and could be effective teachers of their children. This was the focus of the initial Federal grant to Schopler that was the precursor to Division TEACCH in 1966. The Federal grant was enormously successful and had an immediate positive impact on the parents who participated and their children. For this reason, the state of North Carolina adopted Division TEACCH statewide and initiated state funding in its founding legislation in 1972.

Over the past five decades, Division TEACCH has helped to reconceptualise theories about ASD and has created a successful and widely used intervention approach. TEACCH has also implemented a comprehensive service delivery system that has impacted on the lives of people with ASD and their families in North Carolina, the United States, and throughout the world. The programme's major priorities include:

* enabling individuals with ASD to function meaningfully, productively and as independently as possible in their communities;
* to offer exemplary services to individuals with ASD and their families and those who work with them and support them; and
* as a member of the University of North Carolina community, to generate knowledge, to integrate theory with clinical practice and to disseminate information about theory and practice internationally.

Division TEACCH serves people with ASD of all ages and levels of functioning. Starting with diagnostic evaluations that typically occur between the ages of two and four, families first learn about ASD from TEACCH staff, who work out of seven clinical centres geographically distributed throughout the state of North Carolina. Each clinic serves families of people with ASD between the ages of one and 70 in their local regions. About 80 per cent of the initial visits are for children under the age of five.

Division TEACCH integrates a community-based service system into a vibrant university, which encourages the accomplishment of programme goals at a high level of excellence. TEACCH offers the best of what universities are capable of for the benefit of the citizens of the state of North Carolina, including unique opportunities for training, service development and research. The base at the University of North Carolina also allows families easy access to the latest developments in the field and is a wonderful resource for recruiting qualified professionals who often become leaders in the field.

The active involvement of the TEACCH programme in community-based activities also adds to the university's lustre and credibility. By requiring a university faculty to be actively involved in solving day-to-day needs, there is assurance that the programme will not become an ivory tower. Confronting the compelling needs of families and clients with ASD assures that the university-based programme will be working on important and relevant issues.

As part of the state system, Division TEACCH is well positioned to coordinate and collaborate with a variety of state agencies. Transitions from early intervention to school programmes are smoother because TEACCH is available to work closely with each agency and the families. A consistent intervention strategy also facilitates transitions from one programme to the next. Division TEACCH tries to maintain strong collaborative relationships with major state agencies and also the parent advocacy group and service provider, the Autism Society of North Carolina.

Although the statewide system is an important reason for TEACCH's many accomplishments, the programme is not just a coordinating and facilitating agency. Through the experiences of the programme over the past 48 years and with the help of its university base, Division TEACCH has evolved its own treatment strategy and approach to working with clients with ASD and their families. This approach, called Structured Teaching, assures continuity and consistency throughout all of the statewide services for people with ASD and their families.

The strategies and administrative structures from Division TEACCH have been implemented throughout the United States and all over the world. Practitioners and administrators have been using these ideas in each of the 50 American states. Many states have set up TEACCH Structured Teaching educational programmes and there are also numerous clinics and other services following these models. Internationally, these techniques are practised throughout Europe, Asia, Australia and South America and have had a major impact in the UK.

Structured Teaching

The concept of Structured Teaching grew out of Division TEACCH's early recognition of ASD as a developmental disorder (Mesibov *et al.* 2005). When TEACCH was established in the mid 1960s, most professionals viewed ASD as an emotional disorder, caused by parent ambivalence, rejection and inconsistent responses to their children. Eric Schopler, the co-founder of Division TEACCH, was one of the pioneers to recognise ASD as a developmental disorder involving neurological differences from the ways in which typically developing children processed the environment. Structured Teaching evolved as a way of matching educational practices to the different ways that people with ASD understand, think and learn. Structured Teaching is designed to address the major neurological differences in ASD.

Receptive language difficulties are other important characteristics of ASD that Structured Teaching addresses. Many learners with ASD cannot understand language as well as we perhaps think they can, based on their other skills and responses. They also have difficulty initiating responses to our verbal requests. Receptive language difficulties can result in a limited understanding of what appear to be relatively simple requests.

Expressive communication can also be difficult. Language often falls behind other skills for people with ASD so their responses or ability to express simple requests can be limited. Expressive communication requires a degree of initiation, organisation and comprehension that is sometimes beyond what these otherwise skilled youngsters with ASD can produce. This often results in frustration on everyone's part because they cannot express many of their needs in ways that allow others to meet those needs.

Attention and memory can also be different in people with ASD. Although their ability to recall specific details over long periods of time is legendary, working memory, or the ability to process several pieces of information at the same time, is often impaired. People with ASD can have problems attending to the most relevant aspects of situations or to verbal statements that are presented to them. Organisation is another major concern, both organising materials and activities, in both space and time. Familiar material is processed more readily than novelty and there appears to be a strong preference for comfortable activities and routines that have been repeated before.

Other challenges for people with ASD are dealing with other people and also sensory stimulation in the environment. People with ASD do not have an intuitive grasp of others' motivations and behaviours. Social rules are mysterious to them. These can result in inappropriate behaviours designed to gain the attention of other people, social withdrawal, or a preference for being alone. The lack of social relatedness can also make initiatives from other people ineffective in motivating and directing behaviour.

Sensory stimulation can be especially distracting. People with ASD can overreact to stimulation in the environment and have difficulty modulating its impact. Behaviour problems frequently result from their inability to deal with sensory input.

Structured Teaching is a system of organising the classroom and making teaching processes and styles ASD-friendly. Expectations are made concrete and clear to people with ASD. It is a system of structuring educational programmes taking into account skills, deficits and interests of people with ASD. Emphasis is placed on understanding and meeting individual needs, rather than judging student appropriateness or compatibility with some implicit or explicit model of social and cognitive 'normalcy'. For example, many people with ASD have much stronger visual skills compared with auditory skills. Structured Teaching allows them to utilise these strengths by presenting information and instructions visually. Visual information makes things more meaningful for people with ASD and enables them to function more independently and to learn. The main purpose of Structured Teaching is to increase independence and to manage behaviour by considering the cognitive skills, needs and interests of people with ASD and adjusting the environment accordingly. If we are successful in this, the use of Structured Teaching can also facilitate both teaching and learning. There are four components of Structured Teaching that are incorporated into any educational programme: physical structure, daily schedules, work systems, and visual structure and information.

Physical structure

Physical structure and organisation makes the classroom interesting, clear and manageable for learners with ASD. The physical layout of the classroom is an important first step in assuring that a programme will be conducive to the learning styles, needs and sensory peculiarities of learners with ASD. Individual needs must be considered when planning the physical arrangement of the classroom. Where and how the furniture is placed can affect each learner's ability to deal with the environment, understand its expectations and function independently. Clear visual information can reduce anxiety and promote independence. The physical structure of the classroom can also minimise distractions, promoting more consistent and effective work.

Every learner in every classroom will not require the same degree of structure. For learners with ASD who need self-contained classrooms, developing specific areas for specific learning activities, marking clear boundaries, and assuring that materials are easily accessible helps them to know where they are supposed to go and allows them to secure their materials independently. More able learners in mainstream classrooms may not need the same degree of physical structure to direct their activities. For these learners, areas in the regular classroom where there is not as much activity are good to locate and establish as places for them to work. It is usually helpful for them to have a quiet place where they can go from time to time when the noise, visual images and smells of the regular classroom become overbearing.

Ages of the learners will also impact on the physical structure. A classroom with younger learners will need areas for play, independent and individual work, snack, the development of self-help skills, and possibly a bathroom for toilet training. Older learners would need places to pursue their leisure interests, areas for vocational skills, and places for domestic and self-help skills, along with the parts of the classroom needed for independent and one-to-one academic studies, group work and whole-class teaching.

No matter what the level of ability, materials should be clearly marked and arranged at each student's level of understanding. Work materials should obviously be available in learners' academic areas, while play or leisure materials should be available at the time and place where these are appropriate. Easy access to materials at the time when they are likely to be used is important for learners at every age and level of functioning.

For all learners with ASD there are some particularly important considerations in establishing their work areas. This is because of the importance of these areas for developing appropriate independent academic and vocational skills and the difficulty learners with ASD often have in blocking out distractions so that they can focus on the most relevant and important aspects of their tasks. Work areas have to provide opportunities for independent and group work. For learners with ASD who are easily distracted, work areas should be located in the least stimulating sections of the classroom, away from other learners in places with minimal distractions. Some learners with ASD might be able to work next to their peers, but even they may benefit from working consistently in the same place on each of their assignments each day. There should be clearly marked areas to place finished work, even for the most able learners. Easily accessible and clearly marked work materials should be readily available. Additional areas in these classrooms should be established for group work, whole-class teaching, leisure, play, or just relaxation, depending on the needs of the learners.

Often overlooked, the physical structure of the classroom can be an extremely important variable in the success or failure of a learner with ASD. Carefully considering the learner's conceptual and sensory needs can result in a classroom environment that promotes learning and independent functioning.

Schedules

Learners with ASD require predictability and clarity. To the extent that we can meet those needs, we are generally rewarded with calmer and more cooperative behaviour because the learners understand exactly what they are supposed to do. The TEACCH programme incorporates individualised daily schedules as a way of meeting those compelling needs. These schedules, if organised meaningfully with an understanding of each learner's individual skills, can add order, predictability and organisation to their lives.

It has already been discussed how frequently learners with ASD have difficulties with sequential memory and organisation. Receptive language difficulties can also make it hard for learners to understand what is expected, which often leads to their resisting part of the curriculum. Schedules not only direct specific activities as they are occurring, but they also reduce anxiety by helping learners organise, understand and anticipate their daily activities.

In addition to adding predictability and clarity to their lives, daily schedules offer the opportunity for learners with ASD to move around their classrooms and schools independently of adult prompting and direction. This is very important for their feelings of autonomy and also helps them to become less prompt-dependent. Learners who can follow their schedules independently are not as frequently over-stimulated as learners who are constantly prompted and cued and generally confused about where they are going and what is happening.

Checking their schedules regularly can also facilitate transitions, which can be difficult for them. Schedules provide a comfortable, predictable and consistent routine for learners when they are navigating from one activity to the next. They offer a structure, foundation and comfortable routine that helps make the difficult process of changing from activity to activity easier and less anxiety-provoking.

The most typical formats for daily schedules, and the ones that most of us use, are written in the form of timetables and diaries. Our own schedules typically include the entire day. Unfortunately, many learners with ASD have difficulty understanding the written word and cannot conceptualise a full day at a time. For these learners, the schedule can consist of pictures or drawings, representing their activities. For example, a picture of a desk or table can represent their work time; a picture of a swing can represent outdoor playtime. It is also possible to use objects, if these are what the learner most readily understands. Toilet paper for a learner using this system might indicate the toilet, a backpack might indicate it is time to go home, or a floppy disk might be the indication that it is time to use the computer. For learners whose organisational difficulties make a full day hard to conceptualise, their schedules can be presented to them half a day at a time, three activities at a time, or even one activity at a time. The important thing is that the type of schedule and the number of items presented are at the learner's level of understanding.

Work system

The daily schedule is important to indicate the sequence of events during the learner's day. It is a critical factor in keeping learners focused and enabling them to understand what will be happening to them. The schedule is one way of organising learners with ASD in the classroom. Another is the work system, which helps them to organise each specific activity that they are involved with. Work systems have also been referred to as 'activity systems', 'schedules within a schedule' or 'to do lists'. Work systems are critical if learners with ASD are to learn to work without adult assistance or direct supervision. They help learners to know what is expected of them on each of their specific work activities so that they can organise themselves systematically and complete their tasks independent of adult assistance where appropriate. Work systems can also be used to facilitate paired and group learning activities.

Individual work systems communicate four pieces of information to the learners:

1   What work they are supposed to do.
2   How much work (or how many tasks) will be required at this specific time.
3   How they know they are making progress and when they have finished.
4   What happens after the work is completed.

As with effective schedules, work systems are presented visually on a level that each individual can understand and practised regularly until they can be used independently in a variety of settings.

Work systems, like schedules, differ based on the learners who are using them. A written work system might be useful for a learner who can read and understand written language easily, with each task clearly labelled, making it easy to locate. The learner would know what to do by what was written on the work system corresponding to the labels on his work. He would know how much work by the number of items written on the work system for that particular time period. He would also know that the task was completed when each of the written directions was carried out and crossed off. There would also be a written explanation of what would happen after the task was completed.

Written work systems are used for learners who can read and understand language easily; pictures, symbols, numbers, colours or objects can communicate the same information for learners who do not read. A learner at this level might have a work system consisting of different colours arranged as a top to bottom list. Each colour would correspond to a colour label on a visually clear task. The learner would know what task to do by matching the colour on the work system to the work labelled with the same colour. He would know 'how much' by the number of coloured circles from top to bottom. If there were three circles, that would mean that there were three tasks to complete during the work session. The learner would also know that the work was completed when all three of the circles had been removed from the work system. Progress would be understood by seeing each of the circles disappear after each specific task was completed. The consequence for the learner after successfully completing the task could be a picture at the bottom of the work system, indicating what he can do next. The picture could indicate a computer activity or the art area and the child would know to go there after completing the work session.

Work systems help to organise specific work activities. They provide meaningful, organised and effective ways of carrying out specific tasks. They also make the concept of 'finished' concrete and meaningful for individual learners. Understanding this concept gives the learners a feeling of completion and makes moving from one activity to another, traditionally difficult for learners with ASD, a more meaningful process and therefore less anxiety-provoking. Knowing how much work one has to complete and having a sense of making progress towards the completion can be of great assistance to learners with ASD.

Visual structure and information

Up to this point, we have described the organisational systems for moving from place to place (schedule) and for completing specific activities in a variety of different places (work systems). Structured Teaching is also important when thinking about and creating the activities or academic tasks themselves. Each task should be visually organised and structured to minimise anxiety by maximising clarity, understanding and interests. Three components of the activities are especially crucial for achieving these positive results: visual clarity, visual organisation and visual instructions.

Visual clarity

One way of providing visual structure is through clarification. Clarifying important components of a task and essential expectations for learners with ASD can greatly improve their ability to successfully complete these tasks with minimal anxiety. A sorting task can have visually clear shapes or colours and that might help them highlight the essential dimension on which sorting will occur. A carpeted section of the classroom with bright squares might remind the learners that this is the place for their leisure activities. Highlighting relevant and important aspects of worksheets can also be helpful, e.g. highlighting which sentence in each paragraph has the most relevant information or which letter of a word is crucial for alphabetising.

Visual organisation

Visual organisation involves the distribution and stability of the materials that learners use in completing their tasks. Learners with ASD are frequently distracted and disrupted if their materials are not neatly organised and stable. They can easily be overwhelmed, or at least distracted, by sensory disorganisation. Learners with ASD seem to lack the ability to organise their materials themselves so it is essential for teachers and other professionals to order their materials in an attractive, orderly and minimally stimulating fashion. For example, on a sorting task involving a variety of materials, learners with ASD are usually more successful and less anxious if the materials are neatly distributed in cups, rather than spread out loosely on the table in front of them in a big pile.

In addition to neatly organising materials, it is also helpful if large spaces are broken down into smaller components. Learners with ASD have difficulty organising themselves and larger surfaces can compound this problem. A learner washing a large table will probably be more successful if it is divided into four smaller squares, rather than having to take on the entire surface at one time. A complex worksheet may be organised into clear sections to help a learner complete it.

Visual instructions

Visual instructions are the final type of visual structure. Visual instructions are essential components of work tasks. They provide visual information to learners with ASD that explain on their level of understanding exactly what is required for task completion. A common form of visual instruction is a jig, or visual representation, of how materials are to be placed, or how a task is to be carried out. Written instructions can also serve this function, explaining to the student exactly what is expected or required.

Visual instructions are essential components of Structured Teaching tasks for several reasons. First, they help learners to understand exactly what they are supposed to do, a certainty that is essential for most learners with ASD. Visual instructions also allow for a degree of flexibility that is often not seen in ASD. If a learner with ASD learns to complete a task in a specific way, it is usually extremely difficult to alter his strategy or approach to the materials. Through visual instructions, however, we have a mechanism for changing their approach when necessary. Because the learner is responding to the instructions, changing those instructions can alter the responses and result in a learner following a different procedure with the same set of materials. This allows a degree of flexibility that is uncommon in ASD, but essential for effective learning and vocational and community functioning.

Conclusion

In conclusion, the TEACCH programme, now completing its fifth decade as the statewide programme for people with ASD in North Carolina, continues to refine the concept that people with ASD function differently from people without ASD in terms of their thinking and learning and have specialised learning needs, based on these differences. Structured Teaching has evolved as a teaching strategy responsive to these individualised needs that characterise people with ASD. Physically structuring environments, using schedules and work systems, and developing visually clear and organised materials, are the central components of this approach. Learners with ASD who use this approach are calmer, more self-assured and are able to work productively and independently for longer periods of time. The use of Structured Teaching, as a method of delivering the curriculum, can enhance and facilitate the teaching and learning process and can improve access to the curriculum for many learners with ASD.

Chapter 3

Challenges to curriculum access for learners with autism spectrum disorders

Introduction

Learners with ASD share core characteristics (discussed in Chapter 1) that must be addressed if they are to access the curriculum, regardless of what that curriculum is, in a meaningful way. The continuum of characteristics frequently means that learners may not understand or interpret the curriculum in the same way as other learners. Challenges in the areas of communication and social interaction, repetitive and restricted behaviours, activities and interests and, for some, problems with sensory processing, must inevitably lead to consideration of *how* the curriculum is best taught. Traditional teaching styles and curriculum delivery rely on social and verbal communication between adults and children. Meaning in the classroom is derived from a shared understanding of the social context in which all participants need to understand the classroom 'culture'. Learners with ASD often do not understand the shared meaning, explicit or implicit, within the social classroom context. Clare Sainsbury, for example, suggests that such learners are frequently 'oblivious' to the social context of the classroom and recalls her own experience when she felt as if 'everybody is playing some complicated game and I am the only one who hasn't been told the rules' (Sainsbury 2000: 8). This clearly has implications for teaching and learning as the unique characteristics and learning styles of individuals with ASD mean that they think in different ways from those who do not have ASD. Traditional teaching approaches rely upon an understanding of social and verbal communication, but which may not be in the best interests of learners with ASD who are often unintentionally excluded from access to the curriculum.

A 'culture of autism' may be a helpful perspective in reminding us of the need to respect, understand and accommodate their individual differences (Mesibov *et al.* 2005). Consequently, the culture of the classroom needs therefore to reflect their different 'culture' and thinking styles in order to increase their understanding of the classroom culture and meaning of the curriculum.

This book is concerned with facilitating meaningful access to all aspects of the curriculum through the use of Structured Teaching, as created by Division TEACCH (Schopler *et al.* 1995; Mesibov *et al.* 2005). The use of visual structure is now widely recognised as one potentially useful approach to teaching learners with ASD, both in specialist and in mainstream classrooms. Structured Teaching is particularly helpful when considering how best to deliver the curriculum to facilitate access in a meaningful way through the use of visual structure. The approach takes into account our understanding of the characteristics and learning styles of learners with ASD and in particular focuses on areas of strength in visual cognition and the use of special interests to engage and motivate pupils. In addition Structured Teaching is flexible, taking into account both the commonalities and also individual learning needs, together with the differing demands of the classroom contexts in which learners with ASD are found.

The particular challenges to curriculum access and entitlement learners with ASD are the focus of this chapter, with an emphasis on implications for teaching the curriculum. Subsequent chapters provide detailed illustrative examples of how teachers around the world are applying the principles of Structured Teaching to enable meaningful access to the curriculum.

Teaching the curriculum: core principles

The notions of entitlement and access for all learners underpin how we teach the curriculum, regardless of which particular curriculum a school is teaching. For example: the English National Curriculum (Department for Education 2013) states that schools have a duty to respond to pupils' needs and to overcome potential barriers to ensure that every pupil can achieve (p. 9); the International Baccalaureate (IB) (online) states aims to 'create and provide access opportunities' and a commitment to the 'access agenda'. Whilst curriculum content varies internationally, rather than considering the specificities of each curriculum a more useful approach is to consider core principles which are central to teaching the curriculum, whatever the curriculum content and teaching context.

Underpinning values: curriculum, entitlement and access for learners with ASD

Curriculum entitlement and access for all learners is a shared goal, irrespective of which particular curricula is adopted in any particular setting. Jordan (2005) discusses this 'common curricular goal', stating that: 'The child with ASD, like any other child, is entitled to a broad and relevant (not necessarily balanced) curriculum to meet his or her needs, with the issue being one of access' (p. 116). For learners with ASD it may be helpful therefore to identify two aspects to entitlement. First, there is the individual, who has an entitlement to a broad, balanced and meaningful education. Second, there is autism, and the consequent brain differences and individual learning needs that require structure, and in particular structured approaches to enable access to the curriculum.

The importance of promoting access and entitlement to a meaningful curriculum for learners on the spectrum cannot be overstated. In Chapter 1 we indicated that ASD is a continuum with commonality across the spectrum which includes difficulties with social communication, social interaction, and displaying repetitive, restricted interests or behaviours resulting in problems with perseveration and conceptualisation. Moreover, these shared differences and difficulties are displayed in unique patterns of difficulties, differences, strengths and interests in each individual learner. Given the complexity of both common characteristics and the uniqueness of autism for each individual, it should not be surprising to hear that there is no single, simple educational intervention or 'magic recipe' for ensuring learners access curricula. Jones et al. (2008: 15) express a widely accepted belief that:

Given the diversity within the spectrum and between individuals, there is no single educational intervention that is useful for all children on the autism spectrum, and there is no single intervention that would on its own be sufficient to meet all the needs of a particular child on the autism spectrum.... Education needs to be individualised, to allow for different needs and for different teaching goals at different times.

Entitlement and access to the curriculum must therefore adopt an individualised approach, taking into account both the common and the unique barriers to access and learning. Regardless of which curriculum is implemented, if learners are to access that curriculum then consideration of how to teach the curriculum is of utmost importance. The use of innovative and individualised methods of adapting the curriculum, utilising strengths and interests, to make it accessible and rewarding for learners with ASD is advocated by Charman *et al.* (2011: 44). Structured Teaching offers one way of teaching which helps to overcome barriers and promote access to the curriculum by taking into account common and unique needs and differences of learners who are on the spectrum.

Flexibility in teaching the curriculum

A flexible approach to the curriculum takes into account the needs of individuals and in the case of ASD this means adapting teaching styles and strategies to take into account characteristic differences, needs and strengths. The resultant shared and individual needs ultimately mean that each individual will present with diverse learning needs and it is our responsibility as educators to plan diverse ways of teaching the curriculum to ensure access and participation. In addition, those diverse learning needs give rise to potential barriers to curriculum access that require carefully planned differentiation strategies (Rose and Howley 2007). Such strategies are widely accepted in relation to different types of special educational needs, for example using technology to provide access for those who may have motor and/or speech difficulties. In this respect, Structured Teaching strategies for those who have ASD are argued to be equally important in ensuring their access to the curriculum: first by implementing strategies which promote key or transferable skills; second by using visual strategies to facilitate meaningful teaching and learning to ensure greater understanding. It is suggested in this book that for many learners with ASD, more effective teaching can be achieved by the introduction of visual structure that takes into account individual strengths and preferred learning styles. Our intentions, in illustrating the varied applications of Structured Teaching, aim to identify effective ways of teaching the curriculum to maximise understanding. Clearly, the needs of individuals will vary over time and the provision of an appropriate curriculum will need to be considered regularly. However, whatever the priorities for an individual at a particular time, it remains essential to ensure that the curriculum is taught in a meaningful way. Consistent approaches to both teaching and learning are essential to enable individuals to make meaningful progress; Structured Teaching is one approach to developing consistent teaching strategies that are adaptable to differing curriculum content and requirements and that lead to more meaningful curriculum access for individual learners.

Transferable skills across the curriculum

Within any curriculum there exist transferable or key skills which underpin all teaching content. For example, the International Primary Curriculum (online) includes in its 'personal goals' the goal of communication. Such skills are invariably those which present the most difficulties for learners with ASD and which at the same time are priority areas of learning; Table 3.1 summarises the essential key skills which are integral to all aspects of the curriculum.

Clearly the promotion of transferable key skills within any curriculum is entirely appropriate for learners with ASD, however, there still remains the question of how best to teach such skills.

Using Structured Teaching to overcome barriers and challenges to curriculum access

Priority areas of learning evolve from the continuum of difficulties and differences and it is within each of these priority areas that we perhaps most readily see the challenges to curriculum access which are evident every day in the classroom for learners with ASD. Difficulties and difference which may challenge more traditional teaching styles and have implications for teaching different aspects of the curriculum are outlined below. These examples are not exhaustive, rather they illustrate the range of core requirements and skills across a curriculum where learners with ASD may face challenges in relation to curriculum access and where we need to consider

Table 3.1 Key skills and learners with ASD

Communication	All learners need to develop communication skills in order to learn. Difficulties with communication result in significant barriers to curriculum access for learners with ASD across all subjects and curriculum content.
Working with others	Social interaction difficulties create barriers to working with others, including working with adults and with peers in whole class work, group work and paired work.
Problem-solving and thinking skills	Increasing abilities to solve problems and develop flexible thinking are important for all learners. Moreover, developing metacognition or 'learning how to learn' which requires self-reflection is an essential component to achievement. For learners with ASD, rigidity in thinking, together with anxiety, may result in lack of confidence to predict and solve problems, make choices and decisions; in addition, lack of self-reflection creates barriers to developing skills which enhance learning. Moreover because of sometimes extreme anxiety, support strategies are put in place which actually reduce opportunities to learn how to solve problems and develop greater flexibility.
Independence	Independence is essential for all learners. For those on the spectrum independence may be limited due to dependency on others who know them well to act as 'interpreters' and to support their learning. Whilst the role of adults to support individuals is essential, nevertheless the goal of independence is equally important.

how the curriculum is best taught. Aspects of Structured Teaching that may be utilised to build upon areas of strength and address challenges to access are indicated. This leads, in subsequent chapters, to more in-depth consideration and illustrations of curriculum delivery using Structured Teaching.

Begin with building on strengths: visual cognition

Learners with ASD will have a range of individual strengths upon which to build. While the focus is often on areas of difficulty, it is important to identify individual areas of strength in order to facilitate teaching and learning. One area of strength shared by many is the ability to process visual information more effectively than verbal. Grandin (1995: 19) tells us: 'I think in pictures. Words are like a second language to me.' If learners with ASD possess strong visual processing skills and are visual thinkers then clearly these strengths provide us with a useful platform to respond to their diverse learning needs.

Structured Teaching is based on key principles that make use of visual structure. There is an emphasis on developing meaningful learning environments in order to enable individuals to learn. Visual strategies, together with inclusion of individual strengths and interests, provides an empowering approach to developing key skills and to access curriculum content meaningfully.

Communication

Communication is central to effective teaching and learning across all aspects of the curriculum. As all learners with ASD have difficulties with some aspects of communication there are clearly implications for how the curriculum is taught. The teaching and learning process relies heavily on the ability to communicate, and largely upon speaking and listening; for those pupils with ASD we must develop diverse communication systems to increase meaning and understanding.

Structured Teaching builds on visual strengths by first assessing an individual's visual cognition or understanding in order to determine the most effective visual communication strategy. Components of Structured Teaching are then developed for the individual and may include the use of visual schedules, visual instructions and individualised visual communication systems. These strategies enhance our communication to the individual with ASD so that he or she is better able to understand expectations and instructions. At the same time visual communication enables the individual to communicate more successfully.

Social interaction

As with our reliance on communication to teach the curriculum, so we require learners to become increasingly sophisticated in terms of their social interaction skills and understanding. The majority of any curriculum is inevitably taught within a social context which immediately presents challenges to access for those with ASD who are consequently faced not only with curriculum subject challenges but also with challenges arising from poorly developed social skills and understanding.

Aspects of Structured Teaching can be helpful in supporting learners in developing an ability to work with others and can help to structure interactions. For example: physical structure and a work system can be used to support and facilitate working alongside, or playing in proximity to, peers; visual schedules can support and reassure the learner by indicating who they are required to work with and when; visual information can be introduced to clarify the roles of peers and to remind the learner with ASD of the necessary steps for appropriate social skills when working in pairs and groups.

Restricted and repetitive behaviours, activities and interests: thinking skills

Learners with ASD experience difficulties in applying their knowledge in different contexts and generalising their learning. They are often rigid in their behaviours and/or thinking and lack the degree of flexibility required to fully access all aspects of the curriculum. Repetitive behaviours and preferred interests may dominate their thinking, thus restricting access to a broader curriculum. In addition the tendency to remember events or facts without linking their memories to other events and facts exacerbates their poor generalisation skills. The ability to reflect upon curriculum content and their learning is impaired.

Many aspects of Structured Teaching are aimed at developing flexibility, thus allowing the learner to engage in a wider range of activities in varying contexts. The use of schedules may lead to greater flexibility for some and additional individualised visual information can encourage learners to make choices, develop more flexible ways of learning and apply their knowledge and understanding in different contexts. Visual information can be helpful in supporting learners to begin to predict and to identify alternative outcomes to problems; visual cues and structure may also be helpful in supporting and encouraging learners to recall and reflect upon both what they have done and what they have learned.

Sensory processing differences, including hypersensitivities and hyposensitivities, also lead to some of the characteristic behaviours and individuals may become overloaded with sensory information in the classroom environment. Structured Teaching considers the physical structure for each individual and makes adjustments according to needs, for example by reducing sensory distractions in order to create a more effective learning environment.

Attention

Learners with ASD are often described by teachers as being unable to pay attention in lessons, yet at the same time will be overly attentive to some features in the environment. Some will be distracted by sensory stimuli and are consequently unable to attend to the lesson. Learners with ASD may show selective attention, often attending to idiosyncratic stimuli which are more meaningful or interesting to them; they may have difficulties switching their attention from one topic to another and may be able to attend to only one point at a time. This has significant implications for curriculum access as learners are often not focusing on what the teacher requires them to focus on.

The visual emphasis of Structured Teaching approaches can be particularly helpful in enabling those with ASD to attend to relevant aspects of a lesson. Mesibov *et al.* (1997) suggest that individuals with ASD can attend to relevant cues when explicitly required to. The requirement to attend to relevant aspects of a particular lesson can often be made more explicit by visual clarification strategies such as highlighting important and relevant information.

Organisation, planning, sequencing and problem solving

Many learners with ASD show difficulties with cognitive activities such as organisation and planning and frequently do not learn from making mistakes. Cumine *et al.* (2010) suggest that this has a number of implications for planning, self-monitoring, behaviour and flexibility. Poor executive function may help us to understand the difficulties individuals have with organisation and problem solving and may also explain inflexibility, rigidity and impulsivity. Many learners with ASD have difficulties following or devising sequences to achieve a goal. Some individuals may have difficulty remembering everyday sequences, such as the sequence for dressing or cleaning teeth. Many will have difficulties recalling more complex sequences in order to complete an activity, for example carrying out sequences of movements in order to travel across equipment in different ways during physical education (PE) lessons. These difficulties will have implications across the range of curriculum subjects. Visual information can be introduced to help learners begin to follow and understand sequences, beginning with everyday simple sequences and developing more sophisticated sequencing abilities across the curriculum. Such structures will include for example the use of visual instructions using words and symbols to show a required sequence. Later this can be modified to enable the learner to begin to construct sequences more independently within the visual structure provided.

Challenges to problem solving, and the subsequent behaviours which may occur when individuals fail to solve problems, sometimes leads to a reluctance to provide problem-solving activities for fear of triggering behaviours; this may result in lack of opoportunites for individuals to develop the very skills they need in all aspects of their lives and across the curriculum.

A common misconception in relation to Structured Teaching strategies is that visual structure tells a learner what to do and leaves little opportunity for him or her to work out solutions for themselves. Indeed, overly rigid structure may well result in limited opportunities for independent thinking; this is not the goal of the approach. Aspects of visual information may well be helpful in developing abilities to organise, plan and follow sequences of instructions, but also ultimately enabling some to develop strategies to become more effective learners. Providing visual information can scaffold learning in such a way as to enable some learners to independently organise themselves and the way they approach tasks, to begin to make choices and decisions, to make decisions and to solve problems.

Motivation

Many learners with ASD are motivated by very different aspects in relation to learning compared to other learners. The foundation for motivation in schools lies traditionally within a social context and culture. Social motivation has a large role to play for most learners who may for example respond well to verbal praise in front of peers or to competition. The social difficulties in ASD often mean however that individuals are not so motivated by social 'rewards' and teachers need to find other forms of motivation. This particular aspect is not a specific curriculum subject issue but is all-encompassing and will have implications across the whole curriculum.

Structured Teaching taps into individuals' competence motivation by having clear beginnings and endings to tasks and clear visual cues that tasks have been successfully completed, such as the check-lists that often accompany tasks and also the materials themselves which often show a learner that the work has been completed correctly. In addition, the approach places great emphasis on identifying factors that motivate and interest individuals with ASD, including their special interests, and then ensuring that such motivation is provided within a structure that is understood by the individual. Areas of interest may be encouraged in order to motivate learners to tackle areas of weakness, for example using a young child's interest in trains to develop early number skills, or a student's interest in world affairs to develop speaking, listening and debating skills. By incorporating interests and motivators into an overall visual structure learners can be encouraged to take part in curriculum activities that they might usually resist, thus gaining access to a broader range of curriculum opportunities.

Conclusion

There are many curriculum requirements that consequently pose challenges to access for learners with ASD as a direct result of their individual learning characteristics. All types of curriculum should provide a breadth of opportunities for developing knowledge, understanding and skills in priority learning areas associated with ASD and offer a range of meaningful opportunities to facilitate teaching and learning for individuals with ASD. For learners with ASD to gain meaningful access to any curriculum, teaching styles must be a priority consideration. The use of Structured Teaching strategies offers one key approach that allows us to teach the curriculum in a meaningful way to ensure access to breadth of learning opportunities.

Structured Teaching is a teaching strategy for teaching the curriculum, utilising the strengths, skills and preferred learning style of pupils with ASD. It is not a curriculum per se, rather the underpinning key principles can be applied and adapted for individuals in order to access the curriculum. Examples in subsequent chapters illustrate how the components of Structured Teaching are individualised to enable learners to access curriculum subjects, key skills and other aspects of school life such as assemblies and playtimes. Readers are guided to consider the principles underpinning the examples provided – there is no 'recipe' for producing structure due to the diversity of learning styles, strengths and challenges of learners with ASD. Structured approaches must be individualised and therefore will be as different as the learner for whom they are intended. The examples provided are intended to illustrate the flexibility of the Structured Teaching approach and the range of ways the approach can be adapted to enable individual learners with ASD to access the curriculum, whatever that curriculum is.

Chapter 4

Physical structure

Making sense out of the classroom

Overview

Physical structure refers to ways of arranging furniture, materials and general surroundings to add meaning and context to the environment. An effective physical structure helps to decrease the visual and auditory stimulation that can be distracting and troublesome for learners with ASD. It can clarify expectations and activities. A clear and effective physical structure can also add to the learner's sense that the world is neat, orderly and possible to master. This sense is extremely important for learners with ASD if they are to remain calm in school and perform at a level that would be expected given their overall skills.

Clear visual and physical boundaries are a first priority in setting the physical structure of a classroom. These clear boundaries should define the basic organisation of the classroom and minimise auditory and visual distractions. These visual and physical boundaries allow the teacher to define basic teaching areas, such as group work, snack, play, transition, one-to-one work, independent work, whole-class learning areas and 'safe havens' to reduce over-stimulation and anxieties.

In a special school setting, once the physical structure of the classroom is set, the teacher can begin establishing basic routines that allow learners to associate specific activities with specific places. These associations facilitate an understanding of basic classroom activities and expectations. They also make it easier for learners to predict and do what is expected when they are in the designated areas.

Although the classroom environment cannot be manipulated to the same extent for learners in mainstream settings, physical structure is still important. Learners with ASD in mainstream classrooms often have difficulty working independently so the designation and location of an independent work area is crucial. Learners often do better if they are seated near or facing the teacher at a corner of a table, or at the end of a row of desks; easy access to the classroom door may also ease anxieties for those learners who need to leave the classroom for breaks. It is important for learners to understand clear distinctions such as where they work, perhaps with the aid of a work station, and where they can go if they become over-stimulated or anxious, perhaps to a learning support base used as a 'safe haven'.

Physical boundaries are always important for learners with ASD, whether they are in the mainstream or a specialist class. Having adequate space can help them to remain calm and focused on their work. It is important to clarify for learners exactly where they are to be sitting or standing during lessons, especially when they are not at their desks, as lack of physical structure can result in inappropriate behaviour, for example wandering around aimlessly. Distractions and over-stimulation are especially problematic for learners with ASD; having a quiet area in or outside the classroom provides a 'safe haven' to go to which can be very helpful in assisting individuals to calm down when they are becoming upset and to reduce over-stimulation.

Improving physical structure and using routines to increase access to the curriculum

Physical structure is often the first step in increasing access to the curriculum for learners with ASD. In particular, the principles of responding to diverse learning needs and overcoming barriers to learning are critical. For learners with ASD, the classroom and wider school context may be a chaotic environment that causes anxiety and confusion, because of the frequent problems in segmenting and understanding their environment. Many individuals will need a clear, visually organised physical environment as a first step towards increasing their access to the curriculum. By structuring the physical context and creating clear boundaries, physical structure provides one strategy for creating an effective learning environment for learners with ASD. Physical structure strategies are individualised according to assessment of individual needs and may include: discrete working areas for specific activities; reduction of sensory distractions, for example through the use of screens; seating plans; school campus plans which include visually clarified routes between campus buildings.

Without clear physical structure, curriculum access may be limited as learners may resist activities due to confusion and anxiety and/or may find it difficult to transition between activities and classrooms which may result in behaviour management issues. Physical structure is often then the first step in creating a structured and predictable environment, in mainstream or specialist settings. The following examples illustrate how we can begin to create more effective learning environments for learners with ASD by considering different levels of physical structure: defining the purpose of space and reducing distractions within the learning environment. The examples are by no means exhaustive, but serve to illustrate different levels of structure in different contexts, taking into account individual needs.

Case study

First steps: physical structure in a nursery setting

Sam is three years old and has a diagnosis of autism and learning difficulties. He attends an integrated nursery where he is supported full time by a learning support assistant (LSA). Sam has poor understanding of the nursery environment, which his LSA feels is too chaotic and confusing for him. This environment has little meaning for Sam and consequently he spends much of his time running around, frequently engaging in his preferred activities and resisting other activities.

Some structure already exists as the nursery is divided into three areas for discrete activities. The 'red room' is used for creative play, the 'yellow room' is designated as a quieter working area with tabletop activities linked to literacy and mathematical development and the 'green room' is used to promote imaginative play and includes a home corner and dressing up clothes. Access is also available to an undercover outside area for gross motor play. Sam spends most of his time running between the rooms. When he does stop it is often in the creative play room to trickle sand through his fingers. Sam strongly resists joining activities in different areas and his LSA spends most of her time 'chasing' him and trying to get him to stop long enough to look at something with her. Despite the designation of rooms for specific types of activities, Sam requires clearer physical structure to enable him to make sense of the context.

A number of strategies are introduced to clarify the purpose of each area and to reduce Sam's running. Designated space is more clearly defined by using the furniture in the room to clearly demarcate specific areas, for example water and sand are clearly separated from the painting area by a screen (Figure 4.1). This helps to define specific areas for discrete activities and to reduce distractions.

A coloured chair labelled with Sam's photograph is designated as Sam's in the tabletop activities room to indicate that Sam should sit, rather than run. This chair is positioned behind a small table, thus providing Sam with a small, secure area in which to work (Figure 4.2). A bookcase and screen are used to screen his view of the rest of the room, which is highly distracting.

A carpet square identifies Sam's area to sit at carpet time. His square is currently placed on the periphery of the group, with his LSA, where Sam feels more comfortable. At snack time, a tablecloth adds an additional visual cue to help Sam to understand what is going to happen.

Elements of physical structure identify more clearly for Sam the purpose of specific areas of the room and reduce distractions. Combined with the use of basic 'first … then…' routines (see Chapter 5), physical structure is helping Sam to predict what will happen in a given area. This is critical in increasing his understanding and reducing anxiety and has a direct impact on Sam's behaviour and ability to learn. This aspect of

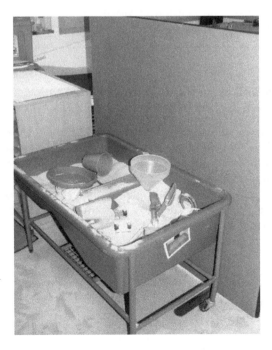

Figure 4.1 Screen used to reduce distractions in a nursery.

Figure 4.2 Independent work area.

Structured Teaching is an important first step in addressing the learning environment for Sam as his access to the Early Years curriculum will be severely restricted if he continues to run around and to resist activities. Supported by physical structure, Sam is working within the personal, social and emotional development aspects of an Early Years curriculum. He is being encouraged to feel safe and secure – a crucial first step to ensure his wellbeing and readiness to learn. In addition, physical structure helps to develop his ability to maintain attention, concentrate, and sit quietly. The introduction of physical structure is coupled with the introduction of visual transition objects to further enhance Sam's understanding (see Chapter 5).

Physical structure and key skills: organisation, independence, managing own behaviour

Key skills which are transferable across all aspects of the curriculum include skills in organising tasks and materials, developing independence and managing one's own behaviour. Many learners with ASD have difficulties in organising themselves and consequently may be dependent upon adults; for example, learners who are easily distracted may never complete a task without multiple reminders and prompts. Adapting physical structure may help learners to develop some of the organisational skills needed for learning and increasing independence and as a consequence some individuals may begin to manage their own behaviour.

Case study

Physical structure in a specialist classroom

The following example illustrates how the use of physical structure takes into account individual needs and can be used in a flexible way. Martin is 14 and is in Year 9 attending a special school for learners with severe learning difficulties. Martin is placed in a specialist class for six learners with autism. He spends much of his time in his base room but also goes to other classrooms for some lessons.

Martin's classroom is divided into areas that are used for designated activities through the use of screens, furniture, mats and coloured tape. Areas are designated for independent work, group work, whole-class activities and leisure (Figure 4.3).

Martin's independent work area is in a corner of the room and faces a wall; a screen divides Martin's area from other work areas. Walls within the area are left blank to reduce distractions, although other areas of the classroom have appropriate displays. Another learner requiring the same level of structure uses this independent area at different times from Martin. The physical structure of Martin's work area enables him to develop organisation and study skills by reducing distractions and clarifying the purpose of the workspace. This enables Martin to concentrate, to focus on relevant information, to sustain his attention for increased periods of time and to begin to work independently.

At group work times, Martin's place is indicated with his name and photograph; these are movable, so that he does not become too rigid about where he should sit. He is often given a chair at the corner of a table with a space next to him to reduce his anxieties when in close proximity to others. When Martin is anxious or distracted by others in the group, he sometimes is helped by the addition of a small screen made from cardboard that stands on his table and divides his workspace from others.

During whole-class lessons, for example literacy, Martin sits on a labelled chair on the periphery of the group. The leisure area is demarcated with bookshelves, a music

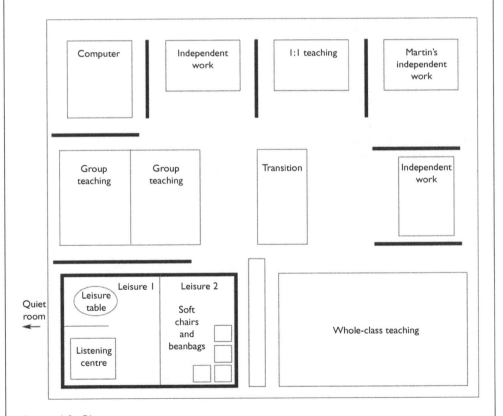

Figure 4.3 Classroom structure.

centre and coloured tape. A soft rug, soft chairs and a beanbag are additional visual cues indicating the purpose of this area. A 'quiet room' is available for Martin (and others) to use when he, or other learners, becomes upset or aggressive; he has been taught to ask to use this at appropriate times. The physical structure provided in Martin's classroom is one strategy for making it possible to teach Martin to manage his own behaviour when anxious, thus developing personal coping skills and independence.

When Martin goes to other rooms, similar strategies are used to enable him to recognise where to sit and to help him to concentrate. For example, Martin particularly dislikes going to the art room as he finds the range of sensory experiences overwhelming. The use of physical structure in this context has been particularly important to encourage Martin to access art lessons. A small room, slightly aside from the art room, is made available to Martin to reduce some of the sensory distractions in the larger room. In addition, because of his touch sensitivity he wears latex gloves when the lesson requires handling of media that Martin finds uncomfortable, such as papier mâché or clay. Martin has also been encouraged to increase his tolerance by introducing different textures very gradually and is beginning to join in part of the lesson in the main room, retreating into the side room when necessary. This strategy is used in conjunction with his schedule (see Chapter 5).

This level of physical structure helps Martin, and other learners, to concentrate, to focus on what is relevant and reduce anxieties. Martin is more willing to join in a wider range of lessons and activities within a more meaningful physical context. Through the use of clear physical structure and the use of 'first … then…' routines (Chapter 5), Martin is able to predict what lessons and activities will be happening in particular parts of the classroom and school, reducing his anxieties and building independent skills.

Physical structure and key skills: working with others

The need to be able to work with others is integral to all curricula; however the nature of the social impairment in ASD inevitably leads to challenges for learners with ASD, resulting in barriers to their successful social inclusion in both learning and in their relationships. The use of physical space and the structure of that space is an important first step in helping learners to interact and work with others.

Case study

Physical structure, working with others and integration

Ricky is six years old, has ASD and learning difficulties and attends specialist provision within a school for children with a range of special educational needs. He attends the specialist class for the majority of his time, but integrates into a Year 1 class twice each week for social activities and structured play. Ricky is very active and flits from activity to activity, sometimes engaging with other children and adults. He is highly distracted, by people and events, and finds it difficult to concentrate. The level of physical structure in the classroom for Ricky is similar to that for Martin. He has an independent work area, defined by screens. The classroom also has a designated play area that includes some low-level physical apparatus, divided from the rest of the room with furniture (Figure 4.4). Two tables at the edge of the play area are used for structured play. Circle

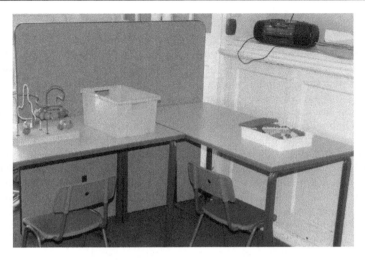

Figure 4.4 Structured play tables in a designated play area.

time and other class activities take place in another defined area using soft chairs and screens to reduce distractions (Figure 4.5).

Ricky's integration with peers in Year 1 is managed with one-to-one support from a LSA. At snack time, Ricky sits with a group of children at the corner of a table. A chair is labelled with Ricky's photograph and name to indicate where he should sit. As he is distracted by most events in the classroom, a small area has been defined in the classroom play area where Ricky is encouraged to join in structured play activities with two peers. A table has been designated for 'structured play' where Ricky is being encouraged to play in proximity with one peer. As Ricky becomes familiar with the physical structure, he can be encouraged to play in proximity to others and join paired activities with peers, developing early skills relating to 'working with others'.

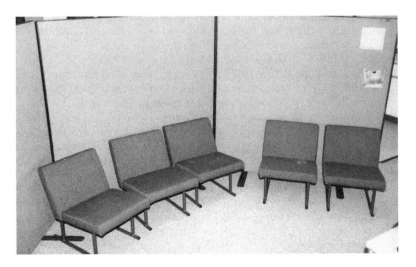

Figure 4.5 Screened area for circle time.

Physical structure at break or playtimes: managing behaviour, communication and making choices

During outdoor breaks or playtimes Ricky tends to run aimlessly around the play areas and frequently wanders into 'out of bounds' areas. The physical structure of the area was not clearly defined and verbal reminders about where to play meant little to Ricky. He was frequently found riding a bike over the field, rather than in the allotted playground. The difficulties Ricky has during playtimes are by no means unique to him so the school has considered a number of strategies to structure the outside areas. A small section of the playground is fenced off to define a smaller area for specific activities. Cones are used to demarcate play areas and a 'road' is painted on the playground to indicate where to ride bikes. The large outside area is now divided into defined areas for discrete activities. This is helpful to Ricky, and to many other pupils, who are beginning to stay in designated areas. As a result of addressing outdoor physical structure, the reduction in running around results in greater attention to activities in each area. As the purpose of space is made clear, Ricky and his classmates are encouraged to make choices about their leisure and recreation time outdoors, the beginning of important communication and thinking skills, Lunchtime supervisors also appreciate the improved physical organisation; their role is more clearly defined as they are responsible for activities in each of the areas. It has been commented that Ricky, and others, are playing more rather than wandering.

Physical structure: transferring key skills to larger spaces

Similar strategies are important when defining the use of space in other large areas. For example, the school hall has three functions: PE, lunch and assembly. Ricky runs aimlessly in the large space, as do many other pupils, and catching them for a PE lesson is almost impossible! Several strategies are used to define more clearly the physical structure of the hall for each purpose. Lunchtimes are not such a problem as the space is more clearly defined by dining furniture. In addition, Ricky has a labelled chair sitting at a table at the periphery of the hall to reduce anxieties among large numbers of children.

The hall has a section that can be curtained off to create a smaller area. When the hall is used for physical education (PE), the apparatus are set up in the larger space and instructions are given in the smaller, curtained-off area to reduce distractions. Benches indicate where to sit while listening to instructions, before then proceeding into the larger area.

When the hall is used for assembly, a layout has been arranged in order to provide consistent cues. Benches, chairs and mats are arranged in a semi-circle and the lighting and putting out of a candle serve as additional visual cues to indicate the beginning and end of assembly. A carpet square is used to indicate where Ricky should sit during assemblies. This is placed at the end of a line as Ricky finds it difficult to sit among a large group of children. However, eventually the carpet square can be moved to different places in the line as Ricky becomes more confident in assemblies.

The physical structure and reduction of distractions is helping Ricky to develop key skills: he is developing essential study and organisation skills as the physical structure helps him to focus and to concentrate by giving meaning to the physical context and reducing distractions; he is being encouraged to stay in designated areas, rather than flitting, in order to help him to learn to work with others and to develop social skills. Simple routines reinforce Ricky's understanding of what will be happening in the classroom and what the expectations are in terms of where to sit and so on. These strategies are useful in the classroom and larger areas, helping to add meaning to the environment. The consideration of physical structure is enabling Ricky to begin to integrate with other children in another classroom, at playtimes, lunchtimes and assemblies. As with Sam and Martin, the understanding of the physical context is further supported by the use of an individualised schedule (Chapter 5).

Physical structure: working alongside peers

Ricky is learning to stay in a space, to tolerate others within that space and to begin to play in proximity within a defined area. Not all learners will require the same level of physical structure as Ricky. However, consideration of physical structure is always an important first step in enabling some learners to share working areas and to work, as well as play, alongside their peers. The following example illustrates the adaptation of physical structure to encourage learners to share working space.

Case study

Physical structure: working alongside others and increasing flexibility

Leila attends specialist provision for learners with special educational needs, two of whom have ASD. This provision is part of a mainstream primary school. Leila is nine years old and has autism and learning difficulties. She is not easily distracted and has good concentration abilities in areas of strength. She has a reasonably good understanding of the classroom context and understands the purpose of designated areas within the room. Leila has an independent work area that is adjacent to another pupil and she is able to work independently within her workspace (see Figure 6.4). Leila spends the majority of her time in the specialist classroom, but also integrates into mainstream classes for some lessons.

In the mainstream classroom, Leila has an independent work area in a corner of the classroom. The teacher has set up two working spaces within this area so that Leila is not singled out. The area is known as 'the office' and children with other special educational needs are able to use 'the office' on a rotating basis. The class teacher has found this to be a useful strategy to encourage children with poor concentration to develop independent work skills, for example during independent work in a mathematics lesson. 'The office' is made available at some times of the day for all children to have the opportunity to choose to work there. Thus the introduction of this physically structured space for one learner has in fact resulted in a useful workspace for many children.

When working within a small group, a strip of coloured tape is used to define Leila's working area on the table. This has reduced Leila's tendency to spread her arms across the whole table, often upsetting her peers. This strategy is also used to define Leila's workspace in other areas, such as the food technology room. In addition, during the whole-class part of a lesson, a coloured sticker indicates Leila's space on the carpet. This has enabled Leila to begin joining the group, albeit on the periphery. As she has become increasingly confident, the sticker is moved around so that Leila does not become too rigid about where she sits. This additional visual cue within the defined carpet area has enabled Leila to begin to sit nearer to peers and sometimes in the middle of a group. The physical structure for Leila focuses on enabling her to share space with her peers, thus laying the foundation for developing her ability to work alongside others.

Developing skills to work with others is applicable in a variety of settings and may lead to cooperative group work. The following example from a specialist setting in India illustrates how physical structure enables four young people to participate in cooperative, vocational group work.

Case study

Physical structure for cooperative group work

Kulpreet, Deepak, Ahmed and Sanjay are young adults aged 18–19 who attend a specialist educational setting for learners on the autism spectrum in India. Kulpreet is 19 years old. He is verbal and interacts with other adults in his environment; he has good motor skills and a good attention span. Deepak is 18 years old and is non-verbal. He gets very upset when he cannot find a particular support assistant. Ahmed is 18 years old and is non-verbal. He dislikes close proximity in the workplace and this sometimes makes him upset. Sanjay is 19 years old; he is non-verbal with poor motor skills and eye–hand coordination. He relies on constant verbal reassurance. They all attend the setting daily and participate in a variety of activities including vocational training. The vocational aspect of the curriculum is a priority, with the aim of preparing young adults to participate in work-related activities in the local community. This case study focuses on adapting physical structure which enables the students to work cooperatively on a shared vocational task.

The teacher has developed a vocational task to develop cooperative group work skills. The setting regularly sends letters, official notices and memos to staff, families and external organisations. This requires a number of tasks which include cutting, stamping and filling envelopes; these tasks are allocated to three of the students, whilst Sanjay is involved in delivering the post to respective departments around school (see Chapter 9 for further information on planning for group work for these students).

A vocational group work area is located in an open space to help the students to become familiar with sounds in the environment and people moving around them. To enable Kulpreet, Deepak and Ahmed to work cooperatively and alongside each other the physical structure is adjusted according to each student's needs. An area of the large teaching space is defined using furniture; individual work tables are placed so Kulpreet, Deepak and Ahmed can sit adjacently in a row; Ahmed is positioned at the end of the row to provide him with greater personal space. Sitting alongside each other reduces the potential pressure of sitting face-to-face but at the same time, the students are close enough to each other to be able to communicate. A small screen positioned on the tables reduces distractions but does not obscure the students' view of others around them; this is especially important for Deepak as he needs to glance around to make sure he can see a particular support assistant.

Sanjay currently needs constant support and while Kulpreet, Deepak and Ahmed work cooperatively he works one-to-one at a work table with a TA. However, he still has a role to play in this vocational activity and, while he does not currently sit near the other three students, the post is placed in a basket for Sanjay; when the post is ready to deliver, one of the students gives Sanjay the basket so that he knows it is time for him to deliver the post (see schedule information in Chapter 5).

The physical layout of this workspace enables the students to follow a cooperative work routine and to develop vocational skills. The physical structure is the first part of the structure which enables cooperative group work; this is then enhanced with the use of schedules, work systems and visual information.

Physical structure: increasing participation in different contexts

The physical structure of a learning environment may be helpful in enabling some learners to participate more fully in different contexts. Learners who are required to move from classroom to classroom may be helped by consideration of the physical structure in each classroom. The following examples illustrate how physical structure can be adapted for individual learners in varying contexts to enable participation in a variety of curriculum activities.

Case study

Emily is 15 years old and attends a non-profit private elementary and secondary learning centre in North Carolina which is geared to children who need structure, consistency, positive reinforcement, more movement, reduced stress, both remediation and challenge along with a multi-sensory way of learning.

Emily enjoys preparing foods, but prefers not to eat any vegetables or fruit. She will say, 'fruit and vegetables make me sick!' In an effort to expand her food preferences, she is taught how to make smoothies using the yogurt she likes and incorporating fruit. In order for Emily to be able to participate in the planned food technology/science lesson, the first step is to set up the physical structure in the kitchen.

The kitchen has four work stations which include stations for washing dishes, watering plants and two cooking stations labelled 'cooking station 1' and 'cooking station 2'. Each cooking station comprises a table facing a wall to reduce distractions while Emily is working.

There is also a 'chill zone' where Emily can choose to go if she feels stressed. In this area, comfortable chairs and access to a computer game help to reduce her anxieties (see Chapter 9 for further examples). The physical structure of the kitchen enables Emily to make sense of the learning space; the use of her schedule, work system and visual information to support access to the lesson are provided in subsequent chapters.

Case study

Physical structure – transition to secondary provision

David attends a specialist school for learners with ASD, he is 11 years old. David is confident within the classroom context and is able to share a workspace, when working independently, with the use of a small, portable screen placed between him and another learner. This is used in a similar way when he integrates into a mainstream classroom and in other classrooms in school.

Plans are being made to prepare David to make the transition to secondary provision where he will be required to move between classrooms for lessons and his working space will change from room to room. His small, portable screen is being used during his visits to the new school to help him to concentrate when working next to a peer.

Despite David's understanding and confidence within the present school building, he is still sometimes distracted. He has an interest in numbers and any displays showing numbers can be highly distracting. This has been addressed by ensuring that David is positioned so that he cannot see distracting displays. Some displays are covered when they are not being used, for example a number line on the wall is covered unless it is time for numeracy. Similar strategies can be used in David's new provision. He is also being encouraged to recognise when he is becoming distracted and to place his portable screen on the desk top to help him to concentrate.

The level of physical structure provided for David has to be adapted for the new school context to enable him to continue to develop his ability to sustain concentration and attention. The use of small, portable screens can be helpful in a wide variety of classroom contexts, including science labs and technology rooms.

Case study

Physical structure in mainstream primary settings

Some learners with ASD attend mainstream schools where it is not always straight-forward to adapt physical structure. Nevertheless, it will be essential to consider phys-ical aspects of the environment to increase meaning and reduce anxieties when necessary. Sarah is nine years old and has a diagnosis of ASD. She attends her local primary school and is supported by a LSA for some lessons. Sarah is generally confident and independent in the classroom and has good understanding of the physical context. She is able to work independently alongside another learner and with groups of learn-ers, with some support from a LSA. While Sarah does not require major alterations or adaptations within the physical space, some issues have been addressed. She uses a desk mat to define her working surface as she becomes distressed if other learners 'invade' her space. Sarah's sensory sensitivity means that she is sometimes distracted by sounds in the classroom, including the ticking of the clock and the hum of the smart-board projector. Sarah always works well away from the clock and is positioned away from the projector when it is used. The teacher also ensures that Sarah has a copy of the image presented on the interactive smart-board to help focus her attention on what is relevant.

Case study

Sofie is ten years old and attends a local mainstream school in a town in Denmark. She is currently in a class of 21 learners and she has five hours of additional support during the week. Sofie is achieving expected levels in all subjects. Whilst she is academically able, she experiences difficulties with organisation and sequencing skills and has par-ticular difficulties with knowing where to focus her attention during taught lessons. Structured Teaching strategies enable Sofie to access a broad curriculum, including the social aspects of school life. Consideration of physical structure in different contexts is important in making sure that every learning environment, including leisure and break times, is effective for Sofie to learn both academic and social communication skills.

Physical structure in the classroom

Sofie has a desk which is located away from windows, to reduce outside distractions, and close to the classroom door should she need to leave. Sofie sits in the last seat on the back row of the class so she can see the backs of all learners; this position reduces the potential stress of not being able to see who is behind her if placed elsewhere and she can also locate the source of noise when seated in this location. This seating position has been found to be the most helpful to enable Sofie to focus on the lesson; the layout and seating arrangement reduce Sofie's anxieties and distractibility which increase her wellbeing and support her so that she is ready to learn.

Physical structure in other contexts: library and computer area

There are two main break times during the day, one of which is outside in the school playground; whilst this is a large school yard, there is a quiet area under some trees where Sofie spends her time during this break. The other break takes place in the computer area which is located in the school library. It is important for Sofie that she has access to a quieter environment for at least one of her breaks as being out in the playground is more difficult for her due to noise, number of people and potentially stressful social demands. During her break in the library, Sofie has a designated place at one of the eight computers which are arranged in a circle; Sofie invites a peer to join her for this break activity – the whole class like to be chosen to play on the computer with her. In addition, visual rules are provided indicating how loud children may talk and how loud they may have the computer volume. This environment provides a quieter and calmer atmosphere than the outside playground.

Physical structure set up to observe peers and activities

Whilst the physical structure of the classroom and library work well for Sofie, there are other activities in school which are more stressful, including for example 'morning song' which is for the whole school. During situations such as this, when individuals on the spectrum may become distressed, overloaded and upset, they may benefit from opportunities to observe the activity for a time before trying to join in. This enables them to watch what happens, but without the added pressure of participating until they are more comfortable with the situation. Repeatedly observing an activity may result in greater understanding of that activity and eventually the confidence to participate. 'Morning song' is recognised as difficult for Sofie, but rather than just withdraw her to another area of the school, instead she sits in an adjacent room which has a window that provides a view of the large room where morning song takes place. From this position, Sofie feels safe and secure and her anxieties reduce; she can see her class easily through the window but does not have to experience the stress of participating. This provides her with multiple opportunities to observe until such time as she feels ready to try to join in; for some learners, arranging physical structure so they can observe activities may be an important first step in being able to access and participate in the curriculum.

Quiet space

Whilst adjustments to environments through consideration of physical structure are effective for Sofie, there are still times when she is overloaded or upset and is not ready to meet the academic and/or social demands of the curriculum. At these times Sofie has access to a small room which contains activities and resources which she likes to play with, for example she plays with Lego, draws pictures and likes to play with dolls, arranging them in different positions. Access to this quiet space is a useful self-management strategy for Sofie which enables her to become calmer before continuing then to participate in lessons.

Case study

Physical structure in mainstream secondary settings

Adam is 15 years old and has Asperger Syndrome. He attends a local mainstream secondary school and is studying for important examinations. Adam has a number of strengths in particular curriculum areas, but despite his good understanding of the physical context in primary school, he has had difficulties coping with the number of transitions in a secondary school setting. For example, teachers allocated seating to pupils each half term and Adam would be unsure where to sit in different classrooms, resulting in anxiety on entering rooms and subsequently at the start of each lesson. It was agreed that Adam could be allocated a consistent place in each classroom, normally in the corner at the front, which he preferred as he could leave easily if necessary. (It had already been agreed with staff that Adam should be allowed to leave lessons and return to the learning support base – a safe haven – when feeling anxious.) Adam is now provided with seating plans for each half term, indicating his place in relation to the rest of the class (Figure 4.6).

Additional visual information also provides Adam with the structure he needs to alleviate his anxieties (Chapter 7). The combination of knowing he can leave, together with the seating plan, alleviates Adam's anxieties to the point where he now stays for most lessons. In addition to seating plans, Adam is also provided with a school campus map which includes visually clear, colour-coded routes to follow between lessons; this visual aid provides a clear plan of the school layout and helps Adam to navigate his way round a large campus successfully.

Adam also experiences sensory disturbance and finds some sounds painful. The school bell, indicating the end of the lesson, caused Adam great anxiety as the sound was painful to him. He spent most of his lessons worrying about when the bell would ring rather than focusing on the lesson content. Adam now has a timer, which he sets at the start of each lesson to indicate a five-minute warning that the bell will soon ring. This allows Adam time to put in earplugs to reduce the painful sensation he experiences.

Consideration has also been given to physical structure during examination periods. Adam becomes very anxious about sitting in the large gymnasium with many learners and this leads to panic attacks before or during the exam. Therefore for all exams Adam is allowed to sit in the learning support base with a smaller number of learners. At these times he is allowed to wear his earplugs to reduce background noise that he finds distracting in a quiet environment. In addition, Adam's noise sensitivity was taken into account when deciding on an appropriate context for his work experience: hence he was placed in a local library where background noise is minimal.

Another area that caused Adam discomfort and anxiety was queuing for a cafeteria-style lunch and eating in the large dining area. Sensory stimulation increased Adam's anxiety in the dining hall, including noise levels and food smells. This has caused Adam to sometimes skip lunch rather than face this stressful context. Although it is not easy to alter the physical structure of the dining area, several strategies have helped Adam to adjust to this context. Adam makes his lunch choice in advance of lunchtime so that his meal can be kept hot. He is then allowed to go to the dining area at the end of the last sitting when he can stand near to the end of the queue, which he finds more comfortable. He is allowed to use his earplugs when the noise becomes too difficult for him to cope with and he is allowed to sit in the same seat each day, at the periphery of the eating area. This is indicated with a 'reserved' label, as used for visitors and others at lunchtimes. When he is feeling most stressed, Adam is allowed to take his lunch to his learning support base.

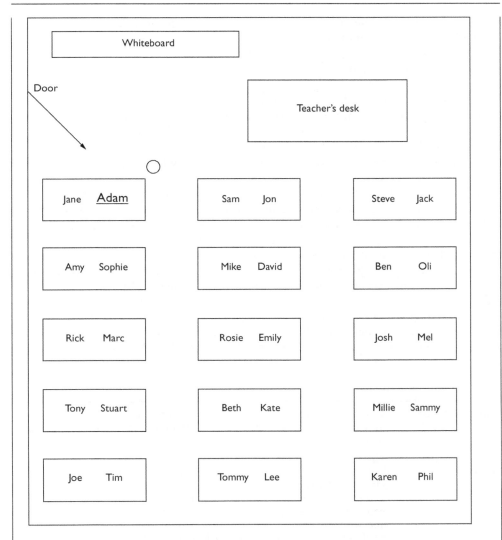

Figure 4.6 Example of seating plan provided for Adam.

Physical structure strategies enable Adam to begin to participate in activities which for him are potentially stressful. By adapting structure to take into account difficulties he has with social interaction, it is possible to reduce anxieties and sensory hypersensitivities; thus physical structure is an important first step in enabling participation in all aspects of school life.

Conclusion

All schools should be working to overcome potential barriers to learning in order to provide opportunities for learners to develop key skills and to access the whole curriculum. For learners with ASD, some of the potential barriers to learning include:

- Lack of understanding of the purpose of the environment or physical context.
- Distractibility within the physical context.
- Difficulties identifying personal space and sharing space.
- Sensory over-stimulation.

These challenges can be addressed, in varying ways, by considering the first level of Structured Teaching, taking into account individual learning needs. By addressing the physical structure and introducing basic routines, learners with ASD can be helped to make more sense of the physical environment and to develop key skills which are essential precursors to curriculum access and which are integral across the curriculum (summarised in Table 4.1).

Adaptation of the environment using physical structure strategies gives meaning to the environment and is an important first step in helping learners with ASD to fully participate and access the curriculum. Requirements relating to physical structure will vary among individual learners and careful assessment of needs informs levels of physical structure necessary for individuals.

Learners who gain greater understanding of the physical learning environment may be enabled to participate more fully. However, while the physical structure provided for a learner with ASD is an important first step to helping them to access the curriculum, further strategies including schedules, work systems and visual information, may enhance participation. Subsequent chapters build upon the foundations of physical structure to further enhance learners' access to the full curriculum.

Table 4.1 Summary of physical structure and key skills

Communication	Communication is supported if learners feel confident, secure and independent. Physical structure is the first step towards achieving this.
Working with others	Physical structure is the first step to enabling learners to develop skills in working and playing with others. Clear boundaries provide clarity and structure in classrooms and outdoors; seating positions and plans give routine and predictability; reduction of distractions reduces over-stimulation which in turn promotes safety, security and wellbeing which help learners to feel more comfortable and confident when required to work with others.
Problem-solving and thinking skills	Physical structure provides information about the learning environment which enables learners to begin to *predict* and *anticipate* activities in particular learning spaces. Being able to predict activities builds confidence and independence, important precursors to developing problem-solving and thinking skills. In addition opportunities to make *choices* can be built into physically structured activities.
Independence	Physical structure may be the first step towards independence, including: developing the ability to understand and navigate the classroom or learning environment; independent transitions between activities, classrooms and outdoors.

Chapter 5

Visual schedules
What's going on?

Overview

Visual schedules provide vital information about sequences of activities, providing information about 'what, where, when and who with'. Daily schedules provide visual cues that tell learners what activities will occur during the day and in what sequence. These cues focus learners' attention on their daily responsibilities and also allow them to predict and understand what will be happening to them and in what sequence. Daily schedules can be developed at any level to match a learner's understanding. The most common types of schedules are objects, icons with written words, pictures or photograph cards, and written schedules. Increasingly schedules are also provided for some individuals on portable electronic devices such as smartphones or tablets. The important priority is for individuals to understand their schedules so that they can use them to move from activity to activity independently.

There are several aspects of schedules that must be considered and adapted for individual learners. First is the level of the schedule, which has already been described (i.e. objects, pictures, words, etc.). This is determined by assessing the individual's level of visual cognition. Second is the length. Possible schedules that can be presented to individual learners include single items, first/then, three or four activities at a time, a half day, a full day, weekly and monthly planners. The questions to ask are can the learner follow a sequence of activities using a visual cue and does the learner understand a 'first ... then...' sequence? If he understands these concepts, then a schedule can contain more than one item at a time.

The way in which a learner with autism uses the schedule is also important. This active involvement can be an effective activity that keeps the individual engaged in classroom activities and also provides a visual message to show the learner that progress is being made and what other activities will take place. Some learners take their schedule words, pictures or objects to the next activity and place them on a matching word, picture or object. Others might turn over their schedule card in conjunction with the activity, cross it off, or place a check mark next to it on their paper. The important priority is that there is a routine method for using the schedule so that the learner is actively engaged as he proceeds from activity to activity. The routine of checking the schedule provides the consistency learners need and leads to greater flexibility in relation to the content of the schedule. Routine ways of checking schedules are taught, taking into account individual needs and cultural factors. Frequently individuals are taught to follow a left to right or top to bottom schedule, reinforcing reading direction. However, learners may also be taught to follow their schedules from right to left if that is the reading direction they are most familiar with or are using. It may be important to check with a learner's family before deciding on the routine as they may have preferences depending upon their situation.

The location of the learner's schedule is another important consideration. For those with severe autism and severe learning difficulties the teacher might bring the schedule information to them, which eliminates a transition, so that they do not get confused by going first to their schedule and then later to an activity. For other learners, there will probably be a transition area on the table or a wall where the individual goes to find out what activity is next. The teacher often uses a transition card, usually displaying the individual's name, when it is time for a transition. The learner takes the name card, goes to the transition area where the schedule is kept, and then proceeds to the next activity as indicated on the schedule.

For some learners the schedule can be portable, such as a clipboard, indicating the daily activities or a regular daily calendar or timetable listing the sequence of activities. Portable schedules will typically be used by more capable individuals in mainstream settings or for learners integrating into other classes or schools. The increasing use of hand-held mobile devices also provides opportunities to develop a useful portable schedule/calendar and organiser for youngsters who are more independent. Indeed, as such devices have become popular with a wide range of people and in a wide range of contexts, this means that an individual with ASD who is using a mobile device is no different to those around him. Teaching individuals to use schedules, calendars and organisers which are available for mobile devices is an effective strategy which is useful life-long.

Schedules allow learners to understand exactly what will be expected throughout the day and to move from activity to activity independently. Schedules help learners to increase their flexibility and can be used to prepare individuals for changes and for 'surprises'. When learners can follow their schedules and consequently understand the teacher's expectations, then changes, when necessary, are also clear to them and much less anxiety-provoking.

Using schedules to increase access to the curriculum

The principle of using schedules, at whatever level, can lead to wider curriculum access in a number of ways. The concept of a schedule is not new to schools; indeed school life relies upon the timetable in order for learners and adults to know what is happening at a given time. However, frequently learners with ASD will find it difficult to follow the general class timetable and therefore require individualised schedules or timetables.

Often learners with ASD do not access all areas of the curriculum due to their lack of understanding of what is expected, for example they find it difficult making sense of everyday events and may not be able to communicate their confusion. This may lead to difficulties in behaviour. Some learners may actively resist some, or even most, of the activities that occur within a school day. Some individuals ask repetitive questions about what is going to happen and become increasingly anxious, their ability to focus on the current activity being impeded by their worries about what might, or might not, be happening later. Often learners are unable to predict the timetable of events, to anticipate and therefore to prepare for activities, or do not cope when changes are made to their routine. This applies to all aspects of the curriculum and may result in barriers to learning which consequently require differentiation strategies in order to facilitate their participation in a broad range of curriculum activities. The use of visual schedules is one such strategy for developing structure and predictability for learners. Individual schedules can provide learners with an understanding of the sequence of activities within a school day. Schedules can increase curriculum access by providing information in a way that the individual understands, thus reducing confusion and encouraging access to a wider range of activities. The use of an individual schedule may help to increase wider curriculum access by:

- improving communication from teachers to learners;
- improving understanding of what will happen, when, where and who with;
- improving the ability to make the transition from lesson to lesson;
- improving the ability to follow a timetable;
- reducing anxiety;
- increasing flexibility and the range of activities a learner is able to access.

Curriculum access depends on developing understanding so that the school timetable becomes more meaningful. It should be noted here that schedules are just one strategy for promoting wider curriculum access. Schedules do not promote greater understanding of lesson content, nor explain how to complete activities, but are critical for improving understanding of what goes on at school. After considering the physical environment, the schedule is often the next step to widening access, participation and understanding.

Schedules are always individualised according to learners' individual needs and cognitive abilities, thus they can be adapted for individual learners in a variety of settings. The following examples reflect the range of schedules and how they can be used to increase curriculum access at different cognitive levels. Examples are provided to illustrate how the use of schedules can facilitate access to the curriculum. These examples are not intended to be exhaustive, rather to illustrate the principles underpinning the approach and the ways in which schedules help learners to access different aspects of the curriculum.

While examples of specific types of schedules are provided to illustrate particular curriculum links, it should be remembered that all levels of schedule can be used in relation to the same curriculum area. For example, the development of aspects of 'personal and social skills' is illustrated through the use of a photograph schedule (see Ricky's case study). This could equally be addressed for another learner using an object, picture or word schedule. The level of schedule used always depends upon individual developmental and cognitive abilities. Careful assessment of understanding determines the level of schedule that provides most independence; assessment is then ongoing in order to determine when learners are ready to move to a different level of schedule. The guiding principle should be to identify the level of schedule that is most likely to increase understanding and independence and to use the schedule, at whatever level, as a strategy for accessing the breadth of the curriculum.

Personal, social and emotional development

Any Early Years curriculum is underpinned by personal, social and emotional development; learning in this area includes children developing self-confidence and motivation in order to be 'ready to learn'. Children who are anxious and confused about the day's activities are not likely to be 'ready to learn'; the use of visual structure and the development of positive routines offer a strategy for developing confidence, understanding and motivation by creating a safe and secure structured day. Some learners with ASD have difficulties moving from one activity to another, partly due to lack of understanding about what is expected. Consequently, he or she may resist joining any activities or may be reluctant to move from a preferred activity. This often causes great anxiety and behaviour that can be difficult to manage and results in restricted experience of the curriculum. Learners who do not understand about the activities in a nursery setting, for example, will not feel confident and may well not be motivated to join in with any activity other than their preferred one. Transition objects may be the first visual cues used to help add meaning and increase understanding for some learners with ASD.

Using objects

Objects are often the first level of visual information that can be used to enhance the meaning of an activity, increase understanding and help learners to make the transition from one activity to another. This is often a first step towards increasing wider curricular access as clearly individuals cannot access the curriculum until they can make transitions without anxiety and can join a wider range of activities, rather than only pursuing their own preferred activities. Once a learner understands that objects represent activities and events and that he can finish one activity and move on to the next, he then has increased opportunities for access. Transition objects can be used in different ways; a child may be given an object to indicate the next activity, and that object is then used as part of the activity, for example a cup indicates snack time and the child has his drink poured into his 'transition' cup. Alternatively objects of reference can be used to indicate transition, but not used as part of the activity; for example a cup indicates snack, but when the individual arrives at the snack area, he places the cup in a 'destination' box and has a different cup to use during snack. Mini-objects and parts of objects can also be used on the schedule, as long as they are meaningful to the individual. Finally, objects may be used that are not necessarily functional or related to the activity they indicate, for example a plastic token used to indicate break time. Assessment of an individual's understanding taking into account developmental and cognitive ability is crucial for establishing which level of object cue is appropriate. Some learners will need to actually use their transition object during the activity in order to gain understanding of cause and effect. Others will understand that their object represents an activity without actually using it. If a learner understands this final type of object cue, he may well be ready to begin using a combined object/picture schedule. The following example illustrates how objects are used to help a learner in the early years to understand what activity is going to occur.

Case study

Transition objects

Sam is three years old and has a diagnosis of autism and learning difficulties. He attends an integrated nursery where he is supported full time by a LSA. Sam has limited comprehension of verbal and non-verbal language but is beginning to respond to single words. Sam has poor understanding of the nursery environment, which his LSA feels he finds too chaotic and confusing. Consequently, Sam tends to seek out his favourite activity, the sand tray, where he engages in repetitive actions sprinkling sand through his fingers and trickling it onto the floor. If Sam is encouraged to join another activity he becomes agitated, putting his fingers in his ears and humming. Sam is severely restricted in his access to all curriculum areas. He will sometimes join in at snack-time, scribble with felt pens and look at a book in the book corner.

One of Sam's immediate targets on his individual education plan (IEP) is to go to, and join in, an activity when directed. This links closely to goals relating to personal, social and emotional development and he is being encouraged, through the use of transition objects, to have a positive approach to new experiences and to be confident to try new activities.

Sam is presented with an object for key activities in the nursery to indicate what he should be doing next. Sam's LSA has identified seven activities as initial priorities, including Sam's preferred activities (sand, books, felt pens and cup) as well as objects for three additional events (outside, toilet and home) (see Table A).

TABLE A

spade = sand	mini book = book corner
cup = snack time	toilet roll = toilet
coat = outside	felt pen = teaching table
school bag = home	

The LSA presents an object to Sam to indicate what he should do; as she gives Sam the object she says one word, for example when giving him the cup she says 'snack'; he is then helped to locate the correct location where the activity takes place, gradually reducing the support until he is able to independently locate each activity.

Sam's transition objects are being used to gradually encourage him to access a wider range of nursery activities by increasing understanding and reducing anxiety. When Sam understands that each object represents an activity or event, he will be introduced to a 'first ... then ...' schedule with two objects indicating the sequence of two activities (Figure 5.1); in this case, a felt pen means 'work' and a cup means 'snack'. Sam will learn to take the first object from the basket on the left when directed, and then the second, to reinforce the concept of **first** you need to do this, and **then** you need to do this.

This level of visual structure establishes useful routines which enable Sam to predict sequences of activities and events and eventually to prepare him for any changes in routine.

Figure 5.1 'First ... then...' object schedule indicating 'first work, then snack'.

Developing communication and early thinking skills

Once learners understand that an object can represent an activity or event, a sequence of objects can be used to provide information about a sequence of activities. Many learners with ASD and additional learning difficulties will not understand cause and effect. Activities in a school day may seem chaotic as individuals have no clear understanding of sequence, i.e. first I do this, then I do that. This often means that it is difficult to engage learners in an activity and then to move them on to another activity when the first is finished. The use of an object schedule will be a successful strategy for some individuals in relation to developing better communication from the teacher to the learner about the sequence of activities, and in developing the individual's early thinking skills.

Communication is a fundamental key skill, essential to participation and achievement in all curriculum areas. Likewise, early thinking skills lay the foundation for the development of future skills which are integral to the curriculum. Early thinking skills include the ability to: recognise and obtain information; predict and anticipate routine activities; understand cause and effect; begin to link events and experiences. For learners with ASD and learning difficulties these skills can present particular challenges. The use of a visual schedule is one strategy that begins to address these areas. The following example illustrates the use of an object schedule that improves communication between teacher and learner and teaches the learner to predict and follow a sequence of activities, subsequently increasing access to a wider range of activities.

Case study

Object schedule

Martin is 14 and attends a special school for learners with severe learning difficulties. He is placed in a specialist class for six young people with ASD. Martin spends much of his time in his base room but also goes to other classrooms for some lessons. He is developing key skills across the curriculum, and has individual targets for communication: one of these targets is to find out what he should be doing and to respond appropriately.

Martin's object schedule improves communication from his teacher to him, thereby increasing his understanding and specifically helping him to follow information. The schedule provides him with information relating to activities that will take place during the school day, enabling him to make the transition between lessons independently. Martin is also developing early thinking skills, in particular those relating to predicting and anticipating activities. He understands that objects can represent activities and has learnt to follow a sequence of up to four objects arranged in a top to bottom sequence.

Martin's schedule is set up by the teacher or LSA for the first half of the morning until break, the second part of the morning until lunch and for the afternoon. Figure 5.2 illustrates a top to bottom, part day object schedule; the basket at the top indicates 'independent work', the plant pot indicates 'gardening' and the cup indicates 'break time'. Martin is directed to 'check your timetable' and takes a transition card with his name on it, matching it to his name at the start of his schedule. He takes the first object and goes independently to the appropriate activity, matching the object to a corresponding one when he arrives at his destination.

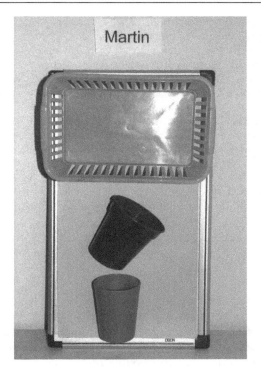

Figure 5.2 Part-day object schedule indicating: 'work, gardening, snack'.

Where appropriate, objects that relate to curriculum areas are used to indicate the activity, for example a calculator to indicate a mathematics lesson or a sports tabard to indicate a PE lesson. Some objects are more abstract, for example red tokens to indicate break time. Martin has in the past been resistant to some areas of the curriculum. For example, he dislikes the smells and feel of some art materials. This causes him great anxiety and he would often lie on the floor and refuse to go to the art room. Strategies have been introduced at a sensory level, slowly building up Martin's tolerance and reducing over-stimulation and distractions (see Chapter 4). These strategies have also been addressed through his schedule. Specifically, it is important for Martin that his schedule contains activities or events that he likes. When art is included on Martin's schedule, it is always followed by one of his preferred activities (e.g. looking through magazines). This helps Martin to cope with attending art, knowing that it will end and that the next activity is one that he will enjoy once art is finished. In this way he is encouraged to attend subject lessons that previously he had resisted.

Martin can now use his schedule to enable him to go to other classrooms and areas around the school independently. As with Sam, this is an important first step to increasing access to the curriculum. Martin understands his timetable and is empowered to follow this independently. As Martin has become independent and confident in the use of his schedule, he is being encouraged to access community activities. Prior to the introduction of an object schedule, Martin would be very anxious about leaving the school building and frequently was left behind when his class went into the community. The use of an object schedule has resulted in Martin joining community activities by increasing his understanding of where he would be going and that he would return to school. Thus Martin is now getting to know a local area and is beginning to use different facilities and amenities in the community, both of which are linked to topic work in geography lessons and can prepare him for the future.

Martin recognises logos from specific shops and places which are also used to support his understanding of his schedule, to support his ability to predict and understand which local amenities his class will be visiting. In addition Martin's teacher is now attaching photographs to Martin's objects as a step towards introducing his schedule in photograph form.

Through the use of his object schedule, Martin is able to recognise and obtain information and is beginning to predict and anticipate activities as he has greater understanding of what will happen, when and where. His teacher's communication is more effective as he now understands daily activities; consequently Martin has developed some independence which raises his self-esteem, crucial for his wellbeing. Martin's access to the curriculum has widened as he begins to participate in lessons that he would otherwise resist and supports him to venture into the community feeling more confident.

Managing behaviour

Whilst schedules communicate the sequence of activities, they are not 'just timetables' and can also help learners in relation to other curriculum aspects. Personal and social skills are critical skills for all learners and the importance of developing such skills cannot be overstated for learners with ASD. Teaching individuals to manage their own behaviour is an essential area to develop and in this respect the use of schedules may enable learners to manage and moderate their own behaviour. For many learners with ASD and additional learning difficulties, their behaviour may seem challenging to others. Frustrations arise due to poor ability to communicate and a lack of understanding of what is happening next. Individuals may develop strong interests, become obsessive and ritualistic, preferring to engage in their own interest and avoid all other activities. This can be exacerbated by a lack of understanding of sequences of activities – why give something up if you do not know when, or if, you will ever get it back? The use of a visual schedule may help individuals to better understand sequences of activities. If pupils know when they will get some time to engage in their preferred activity or interest, they may then be more willing to join in a wider range of lessons and activities. As some learners will recognise and understand photographs and/or pictures, these can be used to increase their understanding of the sequence of events within a school day. The following example illustrates how photographs are used to increase access to a wider range of social skills and structured play activities with peers who are not on the autism spectrum and to help a child to begin to manage his own behaviour.

Case study

Photograph schedule, teaching symbols

Ricky is six years old, has ASD and learning difficulties and attends specialist autism provision within a school for children with a range of special educational needs. He attends the specialist class for the majority of his time, but integrates into another class twice each week for social activities and structured play with peers who do not have an

ASD. Ricky is very active and flits from activity to activity, sometimes engaging with other children or adults. Ricky has some activities that he loves, looking at books being one of these. He is very resistant to stopping his preferred activity and moving on to another, less preferred activity, sometimes becoming aggressive to others if asked to finish; consequently he has limited access to the curriculum.

Ricky was introduced to a photograph schedule in his classroom, the aim being to teach him about the sequence of events in the classroom and to encourage him to participate in a wider range of activities without becoming aggressive to others. Ricky's schedule consists of up to five photographs presented top to bottom on a board on the wall in a quiet part of the classroom. Figure 5.3 illustrates his schedule which indicates circle time, then independent work and then snack. Ricky is given a transition card with his name and photograph to direct him to his schedule. He takes the top photograph and carries it to his destination, posting the photograph in a corresponding pocket near to the activity. He quickly showed that he understood the photographs, so small symbols were added to the top of each photograph in preparation for introducing a symbol schedule.

Ricky's schedule was originally set up to include frequent opportunities for him to engage in his preferred activities, interspersed with short activities in other curriculum areas, thus reinforcing, for example, **first** numeracy, **then** books. Ricky's schedule has had a significant impact upon his ability to take part and focus on activities for short periods and was subsequently introduced in the class into which he integrates. Prior to the lesson, Ricky's LSA sets up his schedule in the Year 1 classroom. It was initially felt that other children might perceive this as strange and might ridicule Ricky. However, the class teacher was delighted to find that other children began drawing and writing

Children more accepting

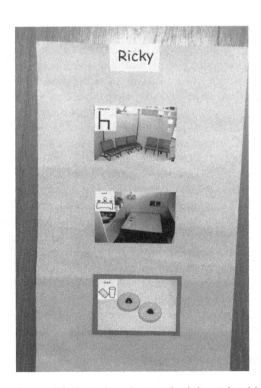

Figure 5.3 Part-day photo schedule with added symbols.

their own 'schedules' for the afternoon, planning activities and making decisions about how to spend their time.

Ricky is learning to use his schedule independently to encourage him to follow his timetable, rather than wander aimlessly, and to increase his understanding of the sequence of activities, thus reducing his outbursts when activities finish. The use of his schedule is one strategy for helping Ricky to gain understanding in order to begin to manage his own behaviour.

Working with others, making choices and decisions, participating in non-preferred curriculum lessons

Working with others is a key skill embedded within any curriculum and important for all learners. Social skills are essential for developing the ability to work with others. Many learners with ASD find these particular skills challenging; for example working with less familiar adults or coping with changes in staff can result in strong resistance to joining in. This is one area therefore that needs to be focused upon in order to help learners to increase their access to the curriculum, particularly where individuals are required to work with different adults for different lessons. The use of a schedule that indicates who the teacher or LSA is, for particular lessons, often reassures learners with ASD; changes are no longer unpredictable as individuals are given warnings through their visual schedules.

Early thinking skills are also important for all learners; for example, being able to recall information in order to remember sequences of activities and/or sequences of steps needed to complete a task. Many learners with ASD will need a scaffold approach to developing these skills, gradually developing their ability to recall information; activities can be added to schedules, thus building sequences which the learner learns to follow and which he can refer to repeatedly to recall the information.

Learning to reflect and improve own learning and performance is another key skill which all learners need to develop. Making choices and communicating preferences are some of the first steps towards developing this skill for learners with ASD who often have difficulties when faced with making even the simplest of choices. Once learners are familiar with and secure in the use of a schedule, choices can be incorporated in order to give opportunities to develop this particular skill.

Learners who are able to follow longer schedules can further increase their understanding of sequences of activities and can begin to make choices and decisions. Such schedules may well address the repetitive questioning frequently heard from learners with ASD about when events will happen. Some may not remember verbal answers to their questions and may be helped by visual reminders through the use of the schedule and other visual cues. Schedules may also indicate with whom a learner will be working, for example which teacher; this may be helpful to those learners who resist working with less familiar adults or who find it difficult to cope when the familiar teacher or LSA is absent. Making choices, learning to remember and working with others are all identified as important skills to develop. The following example illustrates the use of a symbol/word schedule to enable a learner to work with an increasing number of staff, to improve her recall and to make simple choices. Some learners will be able to recognise increasingly symbolic visual information and can use symbols to follow their schedules.

Case study

Part-day symbol schedule

Leila attends specialist provision for children with special educational needs, two of whom have ASD. This provision is part of a mainstream primary school. Leila is nine years old and has autism and learning difficulties. Leila has poor short-term memory and attention span and cannot recall the sequences of activities that take place during the day. This causes her anxiety and confusion and she will frequently refuse to join in some lessons. In addition, Leila is resistant to working with less familiar adults. Consequently she often refuses to cooperate with teachers in mainstream classes and supply teachers. This means that she is unlikely to join lessons not taught by her teacher. Leila's teacher has identified this as a priority as Leila clearly needs to learn to work with a variety of people if she is to access the full range of the curriculum. Finally, Leila shows anxiety when confronted with situations that require her to make choices. Leila's schedule is being used to encourage her to become more independent in relation to transitions between lessons, to work with different adults and to become more confident about making choices.

Leila has a part-day symbol schedule consisting of up to five symbols at one time, presented from left to right on a pinboard (Figure 5.4). This was decided after consulting her parents who felt that while they were familiar with right to left text, they would rather Leila follow left to right and top to bottom information as this is what she is most likely to encounter in her everyday life in the community. Hence, Leila is taught to look for information using left to right or top to bottom routines. Leila's schedule is kept in her work area in the base classroom. She takes the first symbol from her schedule and goes to the appropriate lesson, posting the symbol card into a corresponding pocket when she arrives at her destination. Symbols are usually paired with written words, which may help some learners to subsequently follow a written schedule. The schedule can then also be used as one tool for helping some learners to develop a sight vocabulary, by using familiar words on their schedule. This enables the individual to learn a skill within a functional context, i.e. reading for information.

When Leila is scheduled to work with the regular teacher, a small photograph of the teacher is attached to the appropriate symbol card, thus she knows what she will be doing and with whom. When a different teacher covers the class, his or her photograph replaces the usual teacher so that Leila has some warning that she will be working with someone different. This has proved highly successful and Leila will now work with a number of people, including different LSAs and classroom helpers as long as they appear on the schedule.

When Leila integrates into mainstream classes, she takes a clipboard with a symbol schedule. A photograph of adults in the classroom she is going to is attached to the clipboard. Consequently Leila is able to integrate in the mainstream class and cooperate with different teachers. The schedule has been very reassuring for Leila. She

Figure 5.4 Part-day symbol/word schedule.

uses it independently and is less likely to refuse to join certain lessons. Through the use of her schedule, Leila is also developing organisation and study skills by learning to manage her own time and taking responsibility for completing tasks by following her schedule.

In addition, as Leila's confidence and independence have grown she is now able to make simple choices, hence 'choose' is incorporated onto her schedule. Choices that are available are indicated on a choice board and Leila is being encouraged to make choices during the school day (Figure 5.5).

Making choices is an important skill, but one that learners with ASD often find difficult. Leila is learning to make choices relating to 'leisure and recreational skills'. Making simple choices at this stage, using a choice board, prepares Leila for making increasingly sophisticated choices within curricular areas at a later date.

The use of a choice board can also be an effective classroom management strategy. While some choice boards are used for only one child to access at a time, choice boards can also be used by several children to access within the same classroom. If the teacher does not want more than one learner to have the same choice, only one choice card for that activity is available on the classroom choice board. Equally, if the teacher wants to encourage two (or more) learners to play with the same resources, two (or more) choice cards for the activity can be placed on the classroom choice board. For example, a choice board for young children might include one picture of the train set when there is nobody to supervise two children who may fight over the train! Equally, if the teacher

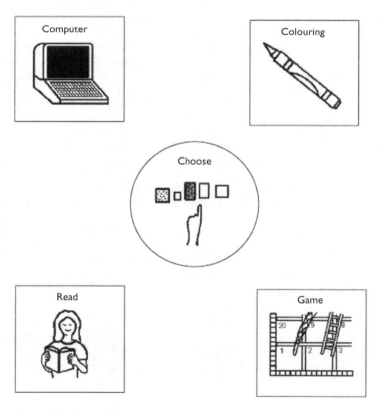

Figure 5.5 Choice board.

wants to encourage two children to play with the train together, and somebody is available to supervise if necessary, two train pictures can be placed on the board.

Leila's schedule helps her to develop a number of skills that are essential to developing independence and promoting participation and learning. She is learning to use a visual strategy to enable her to recall and follow sequences of activities. She is being encouraged to work with a number of adults, by warning her of any changes and enabling her to predict, and she is being given opportunities to develop the ability to make simple choices. A further example below illustrates how the schedule can be extended to meet different individual learning needs and to provide opportunities to increase early thinking skills.

Case study

Schedules to support group work

Kulpreet, Deepak, Ahmed and Sanjay are young adults aged 18–19 who attend a specialist educational setting for learners on the autism spectrum in India. They attend the educational setting daily and they participate in a variety of activities including vocational training.

Individual schedules enable the students to independently follow the sequence of activities each day. Whole-day schedules are provided for all four students and are presented using symbols and words. Photos of the students are added to the group work card for Kulpreet, Deepak and Ahmed to remind the students who they will be working with. The group work post task is included on the schedule after morning break and is followed by a choice of leisure activities; thus the potentially stressful 'group work' activity is sandwiched between snacks and choose (see Figure 5.6). By sandwiching less preferred activities with preferred ones, this helps to motivate students to participate in an activity which requires group work and which is potentially stressful. Sandwiching less preferred activities between preferred ones is a strategy which can be utilised to encourage participation in a variety of curriculum subjects and/or potentially difficult activities.

Sanjay has a 'first, then' schedule, indicating first lunch, then job; after lunch he is prompted to check his schedule and one of the students brings him the basket of mail which cues him to his job of delivering to departments across the school. This example of schedule use illustrates how the schedule can be used to encourage participation in group work; individualisation of the strategy enables some students to have a role in group work even though they are not yet ready to work adjacent to others.

Figure 5.6 Schedule which 'sandwiches' less preferred activity with preferred.

Case study

Stationary written schedule: participating in non-preferred curriculum lesson

Emily is 15 years old and attends a non-profit private elementary and secondary learning center in North Carolina. She enjoys playing games on the computer and surfing the Internet for preferred YouTube videos. Emily is independent in the context of the learning center; she understands her systems well enough that when she becomes anxious or upset, focusing her attention on the schedule or work system to highlight 'what', 'how much' and 'choose' is usually sufficient to help her to stay calm.

Emily is sometimes distracted by worries and anxieties. For example, she worries about whether specific lessons will take place or not. A written schedule is an important strategy to alleviate Emily's worries. The schedule is provided on a clipboard on top of a short bookcase in her main classroom. Emily's schedule informs her of 'what' and 'where'; this information is extremely important in helping Emily to stay focused and calm. Consideration of the individual learner's wellbeing is essential in order to encourage access to a broad curriculum and so Emily's schedule is a vital component of a range of tools planned to enhance her wellbeing (see Chapter 9 for other strategies which support her wellbeing).

Specific lessons are colour-coded on Emily's schedule; the colours match to labelled and colour-coded clipboards which provide the work system for the relevant lesson (see Chapter 7). For example a series of food technology lessons, which also have an aim of encouraging Emily to try new foods, are planned for lessons in the kitchen. 'Kitchen' is clearly identified on Emily's 'Tuesday schedule' (see Figure 5.7). 'Kitchen' is shown in green indicating to Emily that she needs to collect the green clipboard which includes the work system for the lesson (see Chapter 6 for her work system).

Emily's Tuesday Schedule

☐ Check in

☐ Exercise (blue exercise folder)

☐ Work with teacher

☐ Sheraton Café

☐ ??? _____

☐ Work alone

☐ Mailroom (red mailroom clipboard)

☐ Relaxation exercise

☐ Kitchen (green kitchen clipboard)

☐ Social group in library

Next page

Figure 5.7 Written schedule: managing worries and anxieties.

Note that the picture of a rainbow is included on the schedule to make it appealing; as Emily likes rainbows the inclusion of one on her schedule increases her engagement with it. The schedule goes part way to reassure Emily about the day's activities and in particular prepares her for working in the kitchen. Emily is being encouraged to try tasting new fruits during food technology lessons in the kitchen. This lesson has the potential to cause anxiety due to her strong dislike of some fruits, hence the session is preceded by a relaxation exercise and followed by an activity in the library which is quiet and calming. However, it is important that additional strategies are taught for Emily to self-manage her anxieties (see Chapter 9).

Early thinking skills

For many learners with ASD, the development of thinking skills, requiring the ability to reason, enquire and evaluate, is challenging. Those learners who have average or above average abilities in some areas of the curriculum, may still have difficulties in developing these skills. It may be helpful to teach 'early thinking skills', for example, 'remembering' and 'predicting', as precursors to developing more sophisticated thinking skills.

The development of thinking skills is a crucial element embedded within a curriculum. All learners need to 'know how' to learn and for those with ASD, 'learning how to learn' should be incorporated into all aspects of learning. Thinking skills such as reasoning are frequently difficult for learners with ASD and need to be addressed in all areas of a curriculum. Opportunities should be provided to encourage learners to begin to develop their own thinking skills in relation to the problems that they will encounter in their everyday lives. The use of schedules may encourage individuals to develop a problem-solving approach by offering opportunities to make choices and decisions. They can also offer opportunities for learners in specialist settings to participate in integrated activities.

Case study

All day symbol/word schedule

David attends a specialist school for learners with ASD. He is 11 years old and is preparing for the transition to secondary provision. David has good word recognition skills and although he has difficulties understanding fiction, he is able to read directions and to follow written information when accompanied with symbols. He has a number of particular interests including numbers, weather and temperature. David integrates into a local mainstream primary school for some mathematics lessons. David has an all day symbol/word schedule that is kept on a clipboard in the classroom. His schedule is set up for the day and follows a top to bottom, left to right sequence (Figure 5.8). His schedule is generated using the computer and is divided into morning and afternoon. David uses a coloured 'frame' that highlights the activity he is currently doing, moving it down to the next lesson and crossing out the lesson that has finished when it is time to move on. He does not need to carry symbol cards as he is able to remember where to go and is not likely to be distracted on the way to his destination.

Again - know your learner - not one size fits all

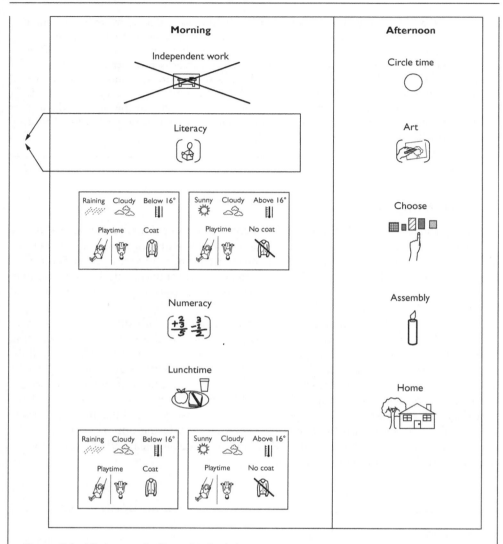

Figure 5.8 All day symbol/word schedule.

David is now able to negotiate some activities on his schedule. He is also encouraged to make decisions and choices about his day as a first step towards developing thinking skills. David's teacher prioritised making decisions as a target for David and decided to link this initially to areas of strength and interests to encourage him to become more confident in making decisions. Hence David's interest in weather was utilised to help him to make a decision about whether he would need a coat at break time or not, something that often worried him. At break times two symbols appear on the schedule: playtime with a coat and playtime without a coat. Each of the symbol cards corresponds to a weather symbol and a temperature indicator (Figure 5.9).

David is encouraged to look through the window at the weather and also look at the class temperature gauge to help him to make a decision about whether or not he needs to wear his coat. Thus the schedule indicates when the break is but also encourages

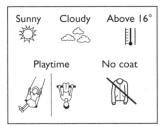

Figure 5.9 Using the schedule to encourage simple decision making at playtime.

David to make a decision about what he will need to wear at playtime. His schedule is helping him to make decisions by indicating alternatives at certain times of the day. David then has to find out relevant information in order for him to make his decision. As well as learning to solve everyday problems, this example also links directly to a curriculum subject, in this case geography. Similar strategies are used to help David to make decisions about what he might need for a variety of activities and lessons; for example a choice of PE equipment for different sports is used to encourage David to select appropriate resources.

Potential barriers to learning could arise for learners with ASD when integrating into a mainstream class. Increased anxiety may result in increased confusion. Learning will not necessarily generalise into a new setting and individuals may feel de-skilled in what may be a more demanding environment. The use of a schedule is one of the strategies that can be used to plan for participation in learning in the mainstream classroom.

When David integrates into a mainstream class for mathematics he takes a portable schedule in a ring binder folder that is set up with the LSA. During David's visits to his new secondary provision, the same approach is used. The need for a portable schedule is important particularly as learners begin to move to different classes and to other facilities within the community; portable schedules can be provided in different forms including clipboards, mini whiteboards, personal organisers, ring binders and increasingly through the use of mobile technology devices such as smartphones and tablets. The use of a schedule is one strategy that helps David to integrate and to participate in a mainstream classroom for some lessons by alleviating his anxieties and ensuring that he understands what will be happening.

Written schedules

Written schedules are used in the same way but allow for increasing flexibility and can be presented in a wide variety of ways. These schedules may look increasingly similar to the diaries, calendars and year planners that we all use in our day-to-day lives. Some individuals with ASD use electronic organisers that incorporate their schedules. As learners become confident in the use of their individual schedules, further strategies such as incorporating a work system (see Chapter 6) can be used to enhance the schedule in order to develop additional key skills. The following example illustrates a written word schedule that enables a learner to recall when events will be happening and an additional class 'diary' highlighting key events of the week.

Case study

Written schedule

Sarah is nine years old and has a diagnosis of ASD. Sarah attends her local primary school and is supported in class by a LSA for some lessons. Sarah has good expressive language, although this can mask her difficulties with comprehension. She has poor organisational and sequencing abilities and asks repetitive questions about the week's events, such as 'Is it swimming today? Are we going swimming? When is it swimming?' Sarah is dependent on routines and becomes anxious when changes are made to the day's activities without warning. Sarah's schedule provides opportunities for negotiation, decision making and problem solving. She is being encouraged to develop early thinking skills by using a visual diary as a reminder for key events. In addition, Sarah is learning to recognise her own anxieties and to develop strategies to reduce that anxiety.

Sarah uses a written schedule, arranged top to bottom in two columns, as a list on a clipboard that she keeps with her (Figure 5.10). Sarah follows the left-hand column of her schedule for the morning, crossing out each lesson or activity when it is finished. She then follows the right-hand column for the afternoon. Sarah's schedule helps her to understand and follow the sequence of lessons throughout the day. She is less anxious about what will be happening and copes with changes to the timetable when they are made clear on the schedule: for example playtime outside can be altered to indoor play if it is raining. Her teacher feels that the reduction in anxiety has allowed Sarah to focus on the lesson, rather than on what will be next. Sarah's schedule also provides a message or reminder that she can refer to throughout the day; this is often a reminder about a behaviour that the teacher is trying to encourage.

Sarah's repetitive questioning about events has reduced as she is now able to see for herself when activities will happen. As Sarah has become confident in her use of her schedule it is possible to add a symbol (?) that indicates that something will happen but we do not know what. This will teach Sarah to cope with unscheduled activities that are part of everyday life.

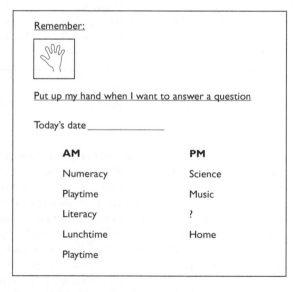

Figure 5.10 All day written schedule.

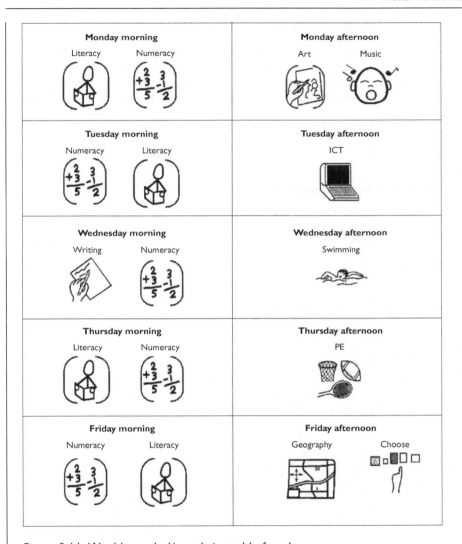

Figure 5.11 Weekly symbol/word timetable for class.

In addition to her individual schedule, a class timetable has been introduced identifying key events for the week. Sarah is referred to this if she asks about events more than once. The weekly timetable incorporates symbols with words (Figure 5.11) as Sarah's anxieties regarding some weekly events lead to her becoming 'de-skilled' in terms of her reading ability. The class teacher introduced this for the whole class as she felt that other children with special educational needs might benefit from being able to see the overall weekly timetable.

Sarah's schedule, together with the class timetable, is providing a tool for Sarah to use in order to enhance her ability to remember, and predict, daily and weekly events. Sarah is asking less often about events, instead referring to the schedule or class diary as appropriate. She is beginning to develop early thinking skills that will serve as a basis from which she can continue to develop her thinking.

Increasingly complex schedules

As learners become independent in their use of a schedule, it may be possible to increase the complexity of the schedule. Note that this should never be at the expense of compromising independence but based upon careful assessment of the individual's understanding of schedule information. The following examples illustrate ways of developing more complex schedules as learners progress.

Case study

Using technology to teach independent use of schedules

Sofie is ten years old and attends a local mainstream school in a town in Denmark. She is currently in a class of 21 learners and she has five hours of additional support during the week. Sofie is achieving expected levels in all subjects. Whilst she is academically able, she experiences difficulties with organisation and sequencing skills.

Sofie has a written schedule to support her understanding of the organisation of the weekly timetable and the sequence of events each day. She is able to independently follow her written schedule, crossing off activities when finished and also updating and amending the schedule to record changes to the timetable. Sofie is skilled at using computers and particularly likes to use a tablet for a range of purposes; this strength and interest has been utilised to teach her how to use an electronic calendar. Sofie adjusted to this new challenge with enthusiasm and quickly learned, with help from a support assistant, how to use the calendar to view the weekly timetable which the class teacher posted each Friday for the following week. Sofie has learned to change the calendar view so she may check the weekly schedule and each day can also be viewed separately. Changes to the schedule are posted by the teacher. Sofie has also been taught to make changes which may arise unexpectedly during the school day.

Sofie's parents, the class teacher and a consultant who has specialist expertise in the autism spectrum all met to discuss how the use of the tablet could be extended as Sofie is highly motivated by the use of her electronic calendar. The autism consultant observed Sofie at school and at home and discussed with the family and school ways which might help Sofie to learn, to relax and to extend her skills. Both school and family agree that Sofie finds it difficult to know what to do at times when she has to wait, for example at school when the class lesson is interrupted and at home when she has to wait for meals to be prepared. It was agreed that activities could be made available on the tablet for Sofie to occupy herself when necessary. Two activity folders were set up, one for school and one for home; the teacher added school-based puzzles and activities to the school folder and Sofie's parents added puzzles, crosswords and other games to the home folder. Sofie's calendar includes a reminder about what to do when waiting: 'If your family needs you to wait at home, please open your home activity folder (green) and choose a puzzle or game. If you have to wait at school, choose a task from your school activity folder (blue).' The same reminder also appears on the daily view of her schedule. This strategy illustrates how the use of an electronic calendar can be extended to include additional features which teach the learner to develop important key skills which will be useful into adulthood.

Problem solving, personal and social education, work-related skills and managing behaviour

The demands of a mainstream secondary school context are quite different from those in a primary school, including a much larger physical context, movement between classrooms and buildings, and larger numbers of teachers. Timetables may be far more complex than those experienced in a primary school. Individuals will need to solve basic everyday problems, which might mean how to find a route from one classroom to another. They will need to cooperate and work with more staff and peers, make choices and decisions and prepare for the transition to the world of work. These demands may well lead to anxiety and frustration, resulting in inappropriate behaviour. The individual schedule will play a critical part in helping individuals to understand, and respond to, these demands.

Key skills relating to problem solving involve learners developing the skills and strategies that will help them to solve the problems they face in learning and life. The individual schedule may help learners to become more independent in solving some of their everyday challenges relating to the timetable, changes to timetables and staffing. Learners with ASD will need to be given opportunities to participate, make choices and decisions, meet and work with people and prepare for change. Increasingly sophisticated use of the individual schedule offers individuals with ASD one strategy within Structured Teaching for developing increasing independence in these areas. They will also need to prepare for moving to college or to work and the use of a schedule will need to be adaptable to these different contexts and will be important in preparing for change. In addition, it becomes increasingly important for learners to manage their own behaviour and to behave appropriately in a wide range of contexts. In overcoming potential barriers to learning, teachers should help learners to manage their behaviour in which case social rules on a schedule may act as reminders of appropriate behaviour. The following example illustrates how the written schedule can be extended to enable learners to become increasingly independent in more complex situations.

Case study

All day written schedule and student planner

Adam is 15 years old, he attends a local mainstream school and is studying for examinations. Adam has a number of strengths in particular curriculum subjects but has had difficulties with coping with the number of transitions in a secondary school setting. In addition, the school operates a two-week timetable system and Adam was often unsure which week he should be following. He frequently became lost on his way to the science labs and was often late for lessons as he could not recall the layout of the building. Adam would become very anxious when late as he likes to be punctual and worries if he misses the beginning of a lesson. Adam is a typical example of a learner who has average to above average abilities in some curriculum subjects, but who has difficulties in other key areas.

Adam has a student planner that provides two timetables, A and B, for his year group like all other students (Figures 5.12a and 5.12b). Adam's timetables have been clarified with room numbers for lessons that are held in different rooms highlighted. He also has a plan of the building that highlights key places in the same way as the timetable.

Week A	8.45 a.m.		11.00 a.m.		1.30 p.m.	2.30 p.m.
Monday	English 101 JW	K	Maths 205 DG | Learning support	H	PE (gym or field– check schedule) AS	PE (gym or field– check schedule) AS
Tuesday	History 115 IP	A	English 101 JW	U	Science L17 AW	Science L17 AW | Learning support
Wednesday	English 116 IP	E	ICT 104 KL	N	Maths 205 DG	Maths 205 DG | Learning support
Thursday	History 115 IP | Learning support	R	Science L14 JR	U	Geography DS	Art A15 MH
Friday	English 107 IP	B	RE 108 MW | Learning support	L	PSHE 101 JW	ICT 104 KL

Figure 5.12a Two-week planner timetable week A.

Week B	8.45 a.m.		11.00 a.m.		1.30 p.m.	2.30 p.m.
Monday	Maths 206 IA	K	English 116 JW | Learning support	H	PE (gym or field– check schedule) AS	PE (gym or field– check schedule) AS
Tuesday	RE 108 MW | Learning support	A	English 101 JW	U	Science L15 AW	Science L15 AW | Learning support
Wednesday	English 116 IP	E	Science L14 JR	N	Maths 205 DG	Maths 205 DG | Learning support
Thursday	Drama studio MH	R	Art A15 MH	U	Learning support	ICT 104 KL
Friday	Geography 108 DS	B	History 117 IP | Learning support	L	PSHE 101 JW	ICT 104 KL

Figure 5.12b Two-week planner timetable week B.

A plan is provided to show the specific route from the room he is in before 'learning support' to the support base as the routes vary between weeks A and B. The initials of teachers are also provided for each lesson so that Adam knows who the teacher will be.

Adam's student planner is currently inserted within a ring binder, divided into week A and week B. Adam has one week to view within his file, the second week is placed within a transparent wallet. Adam changes the week to view on Friday afternoons with the help of learning support. Each week is subdivided into a number of sections including days of the week and homework for each week. The homework section allows Adam to add any extra information he needs, for example hand-in dates and who to hand work in to. This is checked on a regular basis with learning support. Adam has recently included an additional section in which he keeps his 'social stories'.

Adam has a written schedule for each day, which he has learnt to construct himself from the weekly timetable (Figure 5.13). Changes to the timetable are recorded on a whiteboard in learning support so Adam can make sure his schedule is accurate. His schedule also incorporates important 'notices' that serve as constant reminders to Adam. These might include reminders about which sports kit is required for PE, 'social rules' that remind him, for example, not to interrupt but to raise his hand (used in conjunction with a social story) or where to put work that is not finished. Adam finds these reminders reassuring; they reduce the need for him to constantly ask questions to seek reassurance and for the LSA to give verbal reminders that might reduce independence.

Adam can make changes to his schedule as and when necessary. The learning support staff who work with him meet regularly with Adam to discuss any changes to his schedule or week, such as changes in teachers or changes to the timetable. In addition, his schedule can incorporate other important information relating to work organisation (see Chapter 6). Adam's planner and schedule are useful strategies for enabling him to become more independent, to develop problem-solving strategies, to cope with alterations to the timetable and to work with a wider number of staff by enabling him to predict who will be teaching specific lessons.

Adam's school is involved in a number of initiatives to provide learners with a range of opportunities in work-related activities, including work experience and vocational

Monday	Week A
8.30 a.m.	Learning support: check schedule for the day
8.45 a.m.	English 101 (LSA: Mrs Smith)
10.30 a.m.	Break: library or outside
11.00 a.m.*	Maths 207 (LSA: Mrs Taylor)
11.45 a.m.	Learning support – independent study time
12.15 p.m.	Lunch Break: outside or learning support
1.30 p.m.	PE: field, shorts, T-shirt and trainers
3.00 p.m.	Learning support: check homework diary and schedule for tomorrow

Reminders:

Raise my hand rather than interrupt.

Work that is not finished can be filed as unfinished – check with the tutor when to finish it.

Figure 5.13 Written daily schedule incorporating * to show change to timetable and social rules.

courses at a local college. Initially Adam was very anxious about participating in work-related activities but after completing several visits to workplaces he was able to complete a work experience placement in a local library. Adam took a written schedule within the diary section of a 'Filofax' with him to the library; this gave Adam access to the range of information he would need for the placement, including his schedule, incorporating social rules and reminders about expected behaviour.

The schedule is one strategy that enables Adam to develop skills in personal and social education. The schedule provides meaning and security to enable Adam to participate, to make real choices and decisions and to meet and work with a variety of people. Without his schedule, Adam experiences anxiety, which then reduces his ability to participate fully in the breadth of activities provided. Adam is becoming increasingly independent through the use of his individualised planner and schedule. He is beginning to construct his daily schedule for himself by referring to his overall weekly planner. As Adam has become increasingly independent, he is currently being taught to use a planner on his smartphone; this is in preparation for transition to the next stage in his schooling where he will take greater responsibility for organising his time. The school's virtual learning environment (VLE) includes yearly timetables which can be personalised by the student; Adam is learning how to access the VLE and to personalise his timetable to include clearer room numbers for different lessons and reminders about key information and expectations. The advantage of being able to use his schedule in this way means that he can access this information on his laptop, when using a tablet and also on his smartphone.

Conclusion

Schedules are a helpful strategy to enable learners with ASD to understand and follow the sequence of day-to-day events. When a learner can follow a schedule this may facilitate access to a wider range of lessons and activities. The use of visual schedules is one strategy within Structured Teaching for addressing some of the needs of learners with ASD and is an important element within the overall structure that many individuals will need. Schedules are one strategy for responding to diverse needs and providing a teaching style appropriate for those who are visual learners. Curricular access can be improved with the use of schedules for both understanding the sequence of lessons and developing skills embedded within the curriculum. Table 5.1 summarises aspects of access that may be facilitated through the use of schedules.

Table 5.1 Access to the curriculum through use of schedules

Personal, social and emotional development	Schedules promote: positive disposition to learn, self-confidence, motivation. Schedules also establish positive routines and prepare individuals for change.
Key skills	Schedules enhance communication between adults and learners; schedules can support learners to work with others by preparing them for what is expected, e.g. for group work.
Thinking skills	Schedules help learners to: understand cause and effect; recall events and activities; anticipate and predict activities; make choices and decisions. Schedules may also provide opportunities for learners to: solve problems and reflect upon own learning and performance.

The use of individual schedules will require careful assessment, planning, monitoring and reviewing. If we are devising approaches to take into account a visual learning style, it will be necessary to assess individual learners to establish their level of visual cognition. Planning for schedules can be incorporated into individual targets, thus ensuring that progress is monitored and reviewed. Some learners will progress to increasingly complex schedules, others may remain at a particular level; either way, monitoring and reviewing is essential to ensure that the approach does not become stagnant. Essentially, schedules are used that are most functional and meaningful for the individual; the aim is for greatest understanding and independence. It is important that all staff who work with the individual are familiar with his schedule and how it is used to ensure consistency of approach.

While schedules may go some way to helping learners to increase access to the curriculum by increasing understanding of the sequence of activities and developing key skills, difficulties with organisation and sequencing may still hinder learners with ASD. This may include for example difficulties with starting and/or finishing activities, completing activities independently and in groups, following instructions. The next level of Structured Teaching focuses on helping learners in getting organised within a range of learning contexts.

Chapter 6

Work systems
Getting organised

Overview

The individual work system provides learners with a systematic way to approach and organise the work and tasks within lessons. It is a strategy that engages learners with ASD by using their strengths and interests, builds independence, and enables them to generalise their skills into other settings. Complementing the schedule, which outlines the sequence of activities that a learner is to follow during the day, the work system tells the learner exactly what tasks he or she is to complete. The work system is an extremely important and effective way of organising individual activities and tasks within lessons, to give learners strategies for completing tasks and an understanding of important concepts related to their work, such as when their work is finished. Work systems are also commonly referred to as 'activity systems' or 'to do lists'.

Similar to schedules, there are different work systems for learners at different levels of ability. For those with ASD and additional learning difficulties, the work system may be simply organised from left to right. In this case, the individual's work is placed at his left on a single tray or perhaps in individual baskets. The individual is taught to follow a left to right sequence and that the work is completed when everything from the left has moved to a 'finished' basket on the right. Other possible work systems require matching skills to complete tasks in a particular sequence; for example labelling tasks with colours, pictures, symbols and providing a list which visually indicates the order in which the work is to be completed. Alternatively some learners are able to use a written system similar to the 'to do' lists that many people use to organise their daily work. It is also possible to embed a work system into a schedule for learners with good cognitive and conceptual skills.

There are several important ways to individualise work systems, for example in the use of different visual cues or in how the concept of 'finish' is taught. For example: finish can simply mean the materials move from left to right and are placed in a 'finished' box; or tasks and materials are taken to another location in the class-room which is a 'finished' area; tasks are returned to a shelf and are checked off as they are completed. Different systems will be more or less effective with different learners, thus the work system is differentiated according to individual needs and abilities.

For the learner included in a mainstream school, it is especially important that he can identify what work he is supposed to do, and can understand how much must be completed in a specific work period. It is also important for the learner to be able to see that he is making progress as he works and to know when he's finished and also what to do with work that is not finished. Understanding what comes after the work is also important for the transitions that learners in mainstream schools must be able to make, particularly in secondary settings.

Using work systems to get organised

All learners, at all ages, need to develop work, study and organisational skills in the classroom. Curriculum guidance and documentation frequently makes some reference to this area; for example children in the early years, in their personal, social and emotional development are encouraged to show increasing independence in selecting and carrying out activities, be confident to try new activities and maintain attention, concentrate and sit quietly when appropriate. For primary and secondary aged learners, the curriculum includes key skills, including for example, being able to monitor and reflect on their learning in order to improve own learning and performance; young people should be involved in work-related learning and become increasingly independent in a variety of learning contexts.

Learners with ASD face particular challenges in these areas due to poor organisational and sequencing skills, as discussed in Chapter 3. Confusion arises as learners may not understand what work they are to do, how much to do, what to do with the work when it is finished and what to do next. This means some may never begin a task set, or may not know when, or how, to finish. Others will begin, but refuse to finish in the allotted time, not understanding what to do with unfinished work. This may cause extreme perseveration, leading to frustration and sometimes challenging behaviour. Sequencing difficulties may mean that a learner completes one task of several required, but does not complete the whole set. Sometimes a learner does not begin a task, or stops in the middle, because he has no idea how long it will last, or what will happen when it is finished. Tasks can appear to be never-ending; if a learner has an interest or activity that he prefers, he is unlikely to give it up in order to begin something that may never end, with no idea when he might resume his preferred activity! These difficulties are found across the ability range, hence learners with average to above average academic abilities may still have problems with organisation and completion of sequences of tasks, often spending most of their lesson trying to get organised and subsequently not completing the task.

Curriculum access relies upon learners developing organisational skills. Learners are encouraged from an early age to work independently. However, those learners with ASD will be at a disadvantage unless teachers consider their individual needs relating to organisation and sequencing. The use of the work system, as part of a Structured Teaching approach, is one useful strategy that teachers can use to enable learners to fully participate in curricular activities by considering:

- the learning environment;
- organisation and sequencing strategies;
- motivation and concentration;
- communication.

The following examples illustrate different levels of work system, how to use these to increase independent work and organisation skills, how to use work systems across the curriculum, either individually or when working as part of a group, and how to provide opportunities for communication within a work system. Discussion focuses upon organisational strategies provided by the work system. The development of appropriate learning tasks, and how to structure activities within the work system, are discussed in detail in Chapter 7.

Introducing a work system

Work systems are visually structured organisation systems to help learners to complete tasks effectively and to understand the following:

- What work do I have to do?
- How much do I have to do?
- How do I know I am making progress?
- How do I know when I am finished?
- Where do I put the work when it is finished?
- What will I do next?

These are important questions that we all need to address in our daily working lives. Many of us would find it difficult to become motivated by a task that seems never-ending and we often organise our time and tasks so that we have the answers to the above questions. Many learners with ASD do not have access to this information and may be helped by the use of a work system that gives clear visual information relating to the above questions. The use of a work system helps individuals to develop organisational strategies that develop independence, self-confidence, concentration and motivation, and learners may then be able to access a wider number of activities within a lesson.

Early years

During the early years, young children working towards the goals relating to personal, social and emotional development need to acquire a number of basic skills that will become increasingly important as they develop. These include:

- independence in carrying out activities;
- attention, concentration and sitting quietly;
- independence within the environment;
- independent use of resources.

Young children with ASD, and those with ASD and learning difficulties, may have particular difficulties with these areas of learning and may have individual targets to work towards achieving them. The work system is one strategy within the Structured Teaching approach that may help learners to become more organised and independent in their learning.

Case study

Teaching a left to right work system with a 'finished' box

Sam is three years old and attends an inclusive nursery. He is beginning to respond to his physical structure and transition object information and will now sit at a table when given a felt pen. Sam's organisational skills are poor and he has an individual target to complete some activities independently. He is being taught to work independently by completing one activity, provided on his work table. When it is completed (with or without support at this stage) Sam is directed to put it into a large 'finished' box on his right (Figure 6.1). Sam has learnt, through direct one-to-one teaching, to complete some simple activities relating to language, literacy and mathematical development, and also activities to develop fine motor/eye–hand coordination.

Sam is also encouraged to use a 'finished' box when completing other activities such as painting or playing in sand. This reinforces the concept of 'finished' for Sam and helps with making transitions to other activities.

Without a work system, Sam finds the completion of any task difficult; he quickly becomes anxious or overwhelmed by too many resources and frequently either leaves the area, or tips the activity onto the floor. Sam's teacher is responding to Sam's individual learning needs by providing him with an organisational system and routine. Sam is learning to be independent in carrying out activities and is being encouraged to develop attention, concentration and 'quiet sitting' for a short period in order to complete a task. In addition, Sam is learning to become independent within the environment and to use resources independently. The introduction of a work system offers Sam's teacher and support assistants a strategy for giving Sam time to rehearse and consolidate the skills he has been taught, while ensuring that the learning environment enables him to gain independence. As Sam progresses he will begin to use a left to right work system, taking his work from the shelf on the left, to complete a variety of tasks independently (Chapter 7).

Once an individual has learned to use a basic left to right work system with a 'finished' box independently, the system can be extended depending on the learner's attention and concentration span. Learners may begin by completing one task before moving on to the next activity; for example Sam may sort big and little items, place the finished work into his 'finished' box, then play in the sand. Individuals who can concentrate for longer periods may be asked to complete two, three or more tasks before moving on to the next activity. Another way of developing the system is to teach learners to stack their finished work on a shelf on their right, rather than put it into a 'finished' box.

Figure 6.1 Basic left to right work system with a 'finished' box: one task.

Increasing independence, developing personal autonomy and making choices

Many learners with ASD and learning difficulties need to develop organisation and study skills in all subjects across the curriculum, supporting them to complete tasks independently. In addition, individuals need to develop personal autonomy, for example by being provided with opportunities to make choices, for example relating to break time activities. The use of a work system can help learners to develop organisation and study skills, increase independence and offer opportunities for making choices. The following example illustrates these aspects.

Case study

Left to right work system

Martin is 14 and attends a special school for learners with severe learning difficulties. He is placed in a specialist class for six young people with ASD. Martin spends much of his time in his base room but also goes to other classrooms for some lessons. Martin understands the physical environment through the use of physical structure and he uses an object schedule independently. He is able to use a left to right work system in the classroom to complete up to four tasks during a lesson. Martin takes one task at a time from a table on his left and puts the completed task in a filing tray (or a 'finished' box, depending on the task) on his right (Figure 6.2). Two objects are placed in transparent bags on the wall in front of Martin. These objects indicate what he can do when he has finished all tasks. When he has finished his work, Martin chooses his next activity by taking one of the objects; for example he may choose between using a personal music-player in the leisure area of the classroom or using a tablet.

Martin uses his work system for independent working during literacy and mathematics lessons. He also uses his independent work system to consolidate skills that he has recently learned in a variety of curriculum areas.

As Martin is required to work in other areas of the school, he uses a similar work system to help him with organisation. Martin is also able to use this system when working alongside peers in class lessons. For example, he has been taught to 'sort' utensils and rubbish into appropriate containers during one-to-one teaching sessions. Consequently, during food technology lessons, Martin uses a left to right system: his utensils

Figure 6.2 Left to right work system: multiple tasks.

and ingredients are placed in containers on his left and items that are finished with are put into containers on his right (washing-up bowl for utensils, bin for rubbish). As in his main classroom, objects are used to indicate to Martin what happens when the lesson is finished: sometimes this is a choice of two activities, sometimes one object is provided to indicate what's next when there is no choice. The same system is used during art and design and science lessons. Without this organisational work system, Martin would become disorganised and a disproportionate amount of staff time would then be taken up with getting him organised. The use of the work system means that Martin can organise himself more independently during lessons and can consequently focus on the lesson content, rather than trying to organise his materials. He can complete tasks independently and is empowered to make choices, thus developing personal autonomy.

Martin uses his system by taking work from his left in any order. Some learners will be able to match colours, shapes, pictures, letters or numbers and following their system enables them to complete activities in the order that the teacher requires (see Ricky's case study considered next). This allows for the teacher to plan for a sequence of tasks within a lesson or activity.

Extending organisation and study skills, managing behaviour and developing communication

Learners who are able to follow sequences of visual cues to complete several different tasks can develop their organisational skills in a number of ways. The work system can be utilised to increase a learner's attention, interest and motivation, help him to manage independent work time and to complete tasks independently; these skills may lead to an increased ability to manage own behaviour, often a priority area as challenging behaviour may present potential barriers to learning that need to be overcome. In addition, the work system can be used to help learners to generalise their learning into different contexts and can provide opportunities for developing spontaneous communication. Importantly, work systems can also be used during group lessons and for play. The example below illustrates a work system that requires the learner to follow a sequence of tasks in a given order and to use the work system in different learning contexts.

Case study

Left to right colour-matching work system

Ricky is six years old, has ASD and learning difficulties and attends specialist autism provision within a school for children with a wide range of special educational needs. He attends the specialist class for the majority of his time, but integrates into a Year 1 class twice each week for social activities and structured play. Without structure Ricky is disorganised and becomes anxious when trying to find resources, knowing how much work to do and what to do with work he has finished, resulting in aimless wandering and flitting between activities without completing tasks. Ricky uses a photo schedule (Chapter 5) and is able to match colours and shapes. He has been taught to use a colour/shape matching work system (Figure 6.3) within his independent work area and is able to stay on task and to complete up to four tasks during a session.

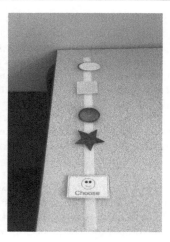

Figure 6.3 Colour-matching work system.

Ricky's work is set up on a shelf on his left, each task labelled with a coloured shape displayed on a pocket. Ricky follows a top to bottom list of corresponding colour/shape cards, placed on a Velcro strip on his desk, by taking the top card, matching it to the corresponding work task and completing that task. He completes all tasks in this way by working his way down his list of colour/shape cards. Completed work is put onto a shelf to his right. Ricky can check his progress and knows when he has finished his work as the colour/shape cards disappear from his desk. Ricky also knows what to do when his work is finished; pinned to the wall are two photographs of activities that Ricky may choose from when he has finished his work. When he has completed all tasks, Ricky makes his choice and takes the appropriate photograph to an adult to request his chosen activity; thus his work system incorporates a meaningful opportunity to develop the key skill of communication.

Ricky uses his work system for independent working during literacy, numeracy and other lessons. This organisational system reduces Ricky's wandering behaviour and helps him to concentrate and to complete tasks. His attention span has increased and he has moved from completing one task to completing four. He is motivated to complete the work for several reasons: he understands the system and routine, he sees he is making progress, and he knows when he is finished and what he will do next. This gives Ricky some control and personal autonomy over what happens to him and increases his self-esteem and independence. Ricky is now beginning to use the work system in other learning contexts, including structured play and group activities.

Structured play

Ricky uses a similar colour/shape matching system for structured play activities in the play area. Without the system, Ricky is less likely to direct his attention to the play materials and more likely to flit around the area. By using the colour/shape matching system with a clear finish, Ricky is enabled to use a wide range of play materials and to complete the activities with support. The system is set up at a structured play table placed at the edge of the play area. Ricky knows what will happen when the play session is finished as a photo is placed on the wall indicating 'what's next'. Ricky's teacher is now developing this to encourage Ricky to play in closer proximity to peers. Ricky uses the work system to find the play activity. He then plays independently, but in proximity to another pupil, with the play materials and places them in a 'finished' container on the right. Later he may learn to play cooperatively with another peer, still using a work system to help him to be organised. The same system is used when Ricky integrates into the Year 1 class where he is learning to play alongside peers within a defined physical area.

Play is not limited to structured sessions, and opportunities are provided to encourage Ricky to develop interactive play. However, the work system is a useful strategy to help Ricky improve his ability to attend, concentrate and to complete play activities with peers, rather than to wander aimlessly. The same system can be used for outside play where activities are set up in discrete areas. For example, each activity is colour-coded and individuals can follow a colour-matching work system to move from one activity to another. In this way, learners can be directed to specific activities and can also make choices as part of the work system. For example, a learner may be directed to the red area for bikes, followed by ball games in the green area, followed by a choice. If the learner likes to wander, this can be included in the choices on offer. Playtimes can then be utilised to teach children how to use play resources, and also to have some free time during which choices can be made. If learners are taught to make their choice, then communicate their choice to an adult, the system thus provides excellent opportunities to communicate. It is important here to distinguish between the schedule and the work system: the schedule tells a learner that it is playtime, the work system (at any level) then helps the learner to organise his time during playtime.

Emphasising 'finished' to manage behaviour

Developing independence and autonomy may facilitate behaviour management and indeed teach learners strategies for managing their own behaviour. Sometimes problem behaviours occur due to poor organisational skills and confusion. For example, prior to introducing a work system, Ricky would often throw materials when he had finished an activity because he did not know what to do with them; the use of a 'finished' container on a shelf or table to his right has reduced this behaviour significantly in the classroom. Hence, Ricky uses a 'finished' container at lunchtimes to prevent him from throwing cutlery and food; a washing-up bowl is placed on a table on his right for Ricky to put all items that he is finished with. Ricky's teacher intends to teach Ricky to take this bowl to the kitchen when lunchtime is finished. The same approach is used in lessons such as art and design, to prevent materials from being thrown.

Ricky has been able to utilise a work system in a number of ways, developing a number of key skills. In particular, he is increasing his capacity to concentrate and complete tasks within different curriculum areas and he is learning to manage his own behaviour more successfully. As he becomes more confident in using the work system, he can approach new activities provided within the same structure, thus beginning to generalise what he has learned. Ricky's structure clarifies the purpose of different areas of the classroom, reduces distractions, lets him know what will be happening through the use of his schedule and helps him to complete work by providing a work system. Further visual information will then help Ricky to understand what he is to do, and how to do it (Chapter 7).

Understand why instead of labelling behaviour

Working alongside others and communication

Work systems are used to enable learners to work independently in a variety of contexts. Some will need to practise independent organisation skills within discrete work areas, away from other learners. However, work systems can also be used to encourage learners to develop their ability to work with others, a key skill required in all curriculum areas. Equally the work system provides an effective strategy for developing communication. Many learners with ASD need to be encouraged to develop their spontaneous communication within naturally occurring contexts. For example, learners with ASD may not ask for help, tell the teacher when they have finished or ask for information; once a learner is familiar with the work system, opportunities can be provided to encourage him to communicate spontaneously.

Case study

Number-matching work system requiring movement around the classroom

Working alongside peers, increasing independence and communication

Leila attends specialist provision for learners with special educational needs, two of whom have ASD. This provision is part of a mainstream primary school. Leila is nine years old and has autism and learning difficulties. She has poor short-term memory and attention span and cannot recall the sequences of activities that take place during the day. Consequently she cannot remember the sequence of tasks she is to complete, she becomes anxious when she does not know what to do and gets very upset when she cannot find resources required for a lesson. In addition, Leila is reluctant to communicate with adults, particularly those who are unfamiliar to her.

Leila has learned to use a work system that helps her to complete sequences of tasks independently. Leila's work tasks are numbered and she follows a top to bottom number list on her desk to complete tasks in sequence. Like Ricky, she takes the top card and matches it to the corresponding numbered task. However, Leila is being encouraged to work alongside peers and to become increasingly independent, so her work is not set up in a left to right system. Instead, Leila fetches work from a shelf within the work area and returns it when it is completed. This storage space is also used by other learners, so Leila needs to ensure that she takes the correct work for her and also has to cooperate with other children who are fetching and returning work (Figure 6.4). Leila knows what to do when her work is finished as a symbol for the next lesson, or 'choose', is placed at the bottom of her number list (this directs her to a class choice board).

The structure provided for Leila encourages her to work alongside peers, in relation to both her physical structure and her work system. She is increasing her independence and is less anxious about getting organised and remembering what tasks she is to do.

Figure 6.4 Number work system, matching to labelled work – shared working area.

remember

**ask Mr Wood
for help**

Figure 6.5 Help card reminder used within the work system.

The work system provides her with visual cues that help her to complete tasks in the sequence required. Without the system she cannot remember the instructions and becomes upset when she has not completed tasks in the correct order.

Leila's work system also provides opportunities for her to communicate with adults. For example, Leila is reluctant to ask for help and will sometimes sit and cry or take her work that is not finished back to the shelf. Asking for help is one of Leila's individual learning targets and the work system is one strategy which is used to provide her with opportunities to request help. Leila's LSA has placed a reminder on Leila's desk and is teaching her to take the symbol for 'help' to an adult (Figure 6.5).

While the majority of Leila's tasks can be completed independently, the teacher has begun to provide opportunities to encourage Leila to seek help from an adult. For example, some of the resources needed to complete a task are missing from the work tray or folder, thus Leila needs to ask for help to find the resources. In this case a similar reminder to ask for help is placed with the task. Reminders can be provided to encourage learners to communicate for a variety of reasons, for example to tell the teacher when they are finished.

Integrating in a mainstream class

Leila's work system provides her with essential organisational skills and with increasing independence she is beginning to work alongside others within a shared space. The same work system is used in the mainstream classroom where Leila works independently at a table adjacent to another pupil. A storage area has been allocated for Leila, but also for other learners to use when they are using the 'office' work station. Other pupils with special educational needs in the class, for example a learner with ADHD, have benefited from the use of the work system approach.

When Leila joins the mainstream class for music lessons, a similar work system approach is used to help Leila to be organised within the lesson. Leila's LSA prepares the system prior to the lesson in collaboration with the music teacher, using numbered symbols to indicate the order of activities such as listening to music, singing and playing instruments. This organisational system means that Leila's LSA can concentrate on supporting Leila with the lesson content and concepts, rather than spending most of the time helping Leila to get organised. While Leila is not expected to complete all of the music-related work independently, she can still use the work system to organise herself and follow the sequence of the lesson.

As Leila develops key skills relating to organisation, communication and working with others, additional visual information is used to extend these skills and to help Leila to begin to develop early thinking and problem-solving skills (Chapter 7).

Generalising skills: work systems in different learning contexts

Work systems are often introduced within one learning context, such as the learner's main classroom or learning support base. However, the work system can also be used within a widening range of contexts as the learner increases in independence and confidence. The following examples illustrate use of a work system in different learning contexts and demonstrate how work systems can be used to teach learners to generalise the organisational skills they have learned by using a work system in an independent work area.

Case study

Emily is 15 years old and attends a non-profit private elementary and secondary learning centre in North Carolina. Emily uses a written, colour-coded schedule which clarifies 'what' lessons she has each day, in what sequence and where (see Figure 5.7). Chapters 4 and 5 showed how physical structure and the schedule help to support Emily to take part in food technology lessons. When those lessons include using food items which she does not like, this causes anxiety and Emily becomes distracted by her 'worries'. Nevertheless, it is important to provide structure to enable Emily to learn strategies to overcome her worries and to take part in a broad range of curriculum activities, including when she dislikes some aspects of a lesson.

Emily checks her schedule which includes colour-coding for each lesson. This directs her to a coloured clipboard which shows a step-by-step written work system for each specific lesson. For example, 'kitchen' is shown in green on Emily's schedule (Figure 5.7), informing her that she needs to collect the green clipboard. Her work system is provided on this clipboard and she then takes this with her to the appropriate location for the lesson, in this case to the kitchen for a food technology lesson (see Figure 6.6).

The work system is an important structure which helps Emily to focus on 'what' and 'how much', and is one strategy which helps reduce her worries. Note that the work system begins with a first step to collect a tablet. As the lesson is likely to cause Emily to become anxious, particularly as she is required to handle fruits which she dislikes,

Emily's kitchen work

☐   Get i-pad

☐   Make strawberry smoothie at cooking station

☐   Remember clean up

Next: choice board

Figure 6.6 Portable work system.

the use of her preference for computers and portable devices is incorporated into the lesson to encourage and motivate her to participate.

The structured work system supports Emily's independence, reminds her of important information to focus on (rather than her worries). The work system enhances her autonomy by including use of a tablet which provides visual instructions to follow during the lesson (see Chapter 7) and a choice of activities when the lesson is finished. This example illustrates how the schedule and work system can be implemented to encourage a learner to participate in less-preferred activities and lessons. This is important in widening access to a broad curriculum; the independence and strategies which structure provides may result in a learner discovering new strengths and interests in lessons that they may well not have participated in without their individualised structure.

Work systems can also be set up to enable learners to work cooperatively. This is illustrated in the following case study which involves learners working on a vocational task.

Case study

Kulpreet, Deepak, Ahmed and Sanjay are young adults aged 18–19 who attend a specialist educational setting for learners on the autism spectrum in India. They attend the educational setting daily and they participate in a variety of activities including vocational training. The vocational aspect of the curriculum is a priority, with the aim of preparing young adults to participate in work-related activities in the local community.

Kulpreet, Deepak, Ahmed and Sanjay are comfortable with the physical structure set up for a cooperative vocational task and they each use their schedules which indicate when they will work on this task and who with. The next step to enable them to develop cooperative work skills is the use of a structured work system. The physical structure is organised so that Kulpreet, Deepak and Ahmed sit adjacently in a left to right row; the work system follows a left to right structure, facilitated by the arrangement of the work tables. The first set of vocational task materials include sheets of letter or memo slips and a pair of scissors; these materials are located in a basket placed to Kulpreet's left so he can easily see 'what work, how much work'. A finished basket is placed to Kulpreet's right for him to put the cut-out slips; the cut-out slips in Kulpreet's finished basket become Deepak's work; Deepak takes the slips and stamps them with the school stamp, placing them in a finished basket on his right. This basket of slips then becomes part of Ahmed's task which is to place the slips into envelopes and place them in a finished basket to his right. Thus the left to right work system provides organisational structure for the three students so that each of them know what work, how much work and where to place finished work (see Figure 6.7). After lunch, Ahmed takes the basket of post to Sanjay, who sorts the mail by colour and delivers them to different departments in school.

The work system provides a structure which enables the students to: (1) follow a work routine as part of a team; (2) focus on the skills needed to complete their part of this vocational task; and (3) communicate with each other about aspects of the task. Kulpreet in particular has become confident in participating in group work and often appoints himself as 'team leader'. For example, he looks to check if the other students are at their places and prompts them if they are not.

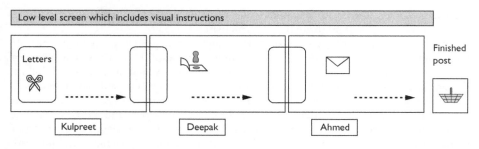

Figure 6.7 Cooperative work system.

This example illustrates how a work system can be designed to support groups of learners to work together (see Chapter 7 for an explanation of the visual information each student requires in order to complete their vocational tasks).

As learners are required to move from lesson to lesson, portable work systems can be set up to facilitate organisation, independence and personal autonomy. As learners develop, they are encouraged to develop confidence and responsibility, to make real choices, to ask for help and to share equipment. The work system can play a role in helping individuals to develop their abilities in these areas that are of particular significance for learners with ASD. The following example illustrates how a work system helps a learner to increase his independence by taking responsibility for organising his work within the structure of a work system, to make choices and simple decisions, to share equipment and to increase his self-esteem.

Case study

Portable number/letter lists, sharing resources

David is 11 years old and attends a specialist school for learners with ASD. He is academically very able and has advanced skills and knowledge in mathematics. He is preparing for transition to secondary provision with the support of a LSA. David follows his symbol/word schedule independently and takes a portable version with him to the secondary school. David's work is kept on a shelf and in his drawer and tasks are numbered or lettered. He uses a number/letter work system in his main classroom, which consists of a list on a note pad. David uses his list to complete tasks in sequence, crossing out each task as it is completed (Figure 6.8). At the bottom of the list he has an instruction to tell the teacher or LSA when he is finished. They can then check his work with him.

A symbol/written card on his desk also reminds David where to put work that is not finished. This is particularly important if learners are not expected to complete the work in one session. Some learners will find this confusing and get upset; in this case a clear place for 'unfinished' work will be as important as the 'finished' place.

The work system helps David to take increasing responsibility for organising himself and increasing his personal autonomy. In addition, David is no longer provided with all necessary materials to complete a task. He is provided with a symbol/word reminder

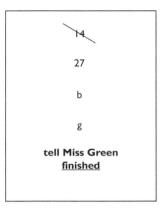

Figure 6.8 Number/letter list to cross off.

within a task that requires him to find the resources that he needs, thus providing the opportunity to make simple decisions relating to his everyday life.

Resources are kept centrally so that all learners may access them when needed. Sometimes David cannot find the resources he needs as other learners have them. A symbol/word reminder placed near to the resources table reminds David to find who has the resource and ask if he can share. Thus David is being provided with opportunities to work towards sharing equipment with his peers.

Integration and transition from primary to secondary provision

When David integrates into a local mainstream primary school for mathematics, and when he visits his new secondary provision, he takes a portable schedule in a ring binder. The ring binder is then also used for his work system. David's folder contains his daily schedule at the front and a note pad for his work system for each lesson. His number/letter list to identify tasks within a lesson is sometimes prepared in advance by the LSA, in collaboration with the teachers, or can be written during the lesson by the LSA.

David follows the list to complete set tasks and to ask for his work to be checked. Clearly this requires preparation and collaboration between David's LSA and his teachers. Sometimes information is not available until the lesson, or requirements change. The LSA can produce, add to or amend David's list during the lesson if required. In addition, the teacher sometimes offers a choice in relation to the order in which tasks should be completed and in this case David's list will indicate where there is a choice (Figure 6.9). This provides opportunities for David to make simple decisions and to solve simple everyday problems. For example, he may choose a particular task because the resources he needs for the other task are being used. He can then negotiate to use them after the other learner has finished with them. In the meantime he can get on with another task.

David is using a work system strategy for independent work, but also within lessons when he might need support. As with Leila, a LSA then spends time more productively supporting David with lesson concepts when required. Thus he can still find the work for himself, he knows in what order to complete it and he knows what to do when it is finished. He is moving independently to a number of places to find and return work and he is beginning to share resources. David is taking responsibility for himself, making choices and developing independence. His work system is

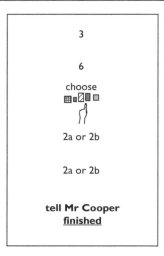

Figure 6.9 Number/letter list with choice of order of tasks.

not dissimilar to the lists many of us set up for ourselves when faced with a large number of tasks to complete.

Work systems in inclusive settings: working with others

Work systems can be useful in inclusive classrooms and may provide a useful differentiation strategy to help a learner to be included. Some with ASD will find the organisational requirements in a mainstream classroom stressful and overwhelming. This may lead to inappropriate behaviours such as work refusal or avoidance, aggression or excessive anxiety that may put at risk their ability to be included. LSAs may find themselves spending considerable time supporting the learner in relation to his organisational difficulties and valuable time is lost for concentrating on learning lesson concepts. The use of a work system may help the learner to overcome difficulties with organisation, possibly reducing or removing a potential barrier to learning. The work system provides one strategy for enabling learners to be included by empowering individuals to organise themselves within a mainstream context. The work system can be used to facilitate independent working but can also be used within lessons where a learner may need support. In addition, while work systems are often effective in facilitating individual working, they can also be used to develop abilities to work with others. The following example is illustrative of a work system that is flexible and used in a variety of contexts for independent and cooperative work.

Case study

Written work systems

Developing independence and flexibility

Sarah is 9 years old and has a diagnosis of ASD. She attends her local primary school and is supported by a LSA for some lessons. Sarah has good expressive language, although this can mask her difficulties with comprehension. She has poor organisational and sequencing abilities and is unable to recall sequences of instructions. Sarah uses a written, daily schedule (Chapter 5) and is also helped with additional symbols when needed, for example at times of anxiety.

Sarah uses a work system that combines number and written instructions. Her work system is contained in a filing box, divided into lessons (Figure 6.10). Sarah finds the appropriate file card for the lesson and checks off each task as it is completed. Sarah knows 'what's next' from a written statement at the end of her final task. Sarah's work system indicates what work she is to do and in what order to complete the tasks.

The LSA usually prepares the work system for specific lessons, including literacy and numeracy, after consulting the teacher to find out what Sarah is to do. The LSA is given time to prepare Sarah's work system for the following day's lessons during the final part of the afternoon. The LSA has prepared a variety of numbered and written cards that are laminated and can be reused. In addition, a number of cards are blank so that the LSA can indicate new tasks during a lesson. Sarah is being encouraged to listen to the teacher's verbal instructions and to write them onto her work system for herself; this is helped by teachers who provide instructions for the class on the smartboard.

Sarah knows what work to do, how much she has to do and what happens when she has finished. She is able to cope with alterations to her work system and will amend instructions herself when directed. Also she is learning to cope when, for example, there is no time to complete a task and will cross it off from her list when asked to.

Sarah's work system enables her to be independent in relation to organisation. Without the system, Sarah would become confused and distressed and would often be taken out of the lesson by the LSA to calm down. Consequently she would miss some of the lesson and this would add to her distress. Sarah's number/written work system is quick and easy to produce, yet is empowering for Sarah in relation to developing independence and helping her to be included.

Sarah uses her work system for most lessons. This enables her to be organised in a range of subject areas. In addition to using her system for independent working, she also refers to it when working with a small group. This has been developed to encourage Sarah

Figure 6.10 Work system in filing box.

to cooperate with other learners in group tasks. For example, Sarah's class prepared a report for a school newsletter about their recent sports day, focusing on writing, speaking and listening and ICT. A 'jigsaw' approach (see Chapter 9 for an example) was used to divide several tasks between groups. Tasks included:

- interviewing learners to identify quotes and sub-headings for the report;
- writing the report;
- sorting, selecting and preparing photographs, which were taken with a digital camera during the event, in order to prepare a photograph collage, with captions.

All learners worked together on editing and preparing the final report. Sarah's individual objectives were to make choices of pictures, to discuss reasons for her choices with two other learners, to write captions and to share and take turns in discussing photographs. Sarah's work system indicates her tasks but also reminds her of her peers' tasks (Figure 6.11). Additional written instructions were provided for Sarah in order for her to use the software appropriately (Chapter 7).

Each group reported to the class on what they had done, and why they had done it that way. Sarah's work system card helped her to recall what her group had done and to tell the class, thus offering an opportunity for her to reflect upon and evaluate the group's activity as part of their work on key skills.

Sarah's work system enables her to cooperate with her peers and be successful in completing her part of the task. The combination of a work system within a jigsaw approach is sometimes a useful strategy for helping learners with ASD to be included in group tasks (Howley and Rose 2003). Learners can be allocated a part of the task that is most likely to interest them, or that uses their strengths, and the work system is used to help with understanding what they have to do, how much and what to do when finished. While Sarah can work alongside her peers, some with ASD are not yet able to do so. Nevertheless they may be included in the lesson by being allocated a part of the task and completing it at their independent work station, using their work system. They can then make their contribution to the final piece of work.

Sarah is using her work system to complete activities independently and to work with others in a group activity.

English and ICT
Preparing a newsletter report

1. Whole class: listen ☐

2. Group 1
   - select photos ☐
   - Jane choose 2 ☐
     (Sarah listen)
   - Sarah choose 2
     tell others why you ☐
     have chosen
   - Jack choose 2 ☐
     (Sarah listen)

3. Organise layout together ☐

4. Write captions ☐

5. Whole class edit report
   Sarah listen then tell class ☐
   what the group has done

6. Check your schedule ☐

Figure 6.11 Work system in a group activity.

It is important that work systems are also used to help learners to understand the organisation and sequence of whole-class lessons. The following example illustrates how a written work system can support a learner to follow the organisation of class lessons.

Case study

Written work system and instructions

Sofie is ten years old and attends a local mainstream school in a town in Denmark. She is currently in a class of 21 learners and she has five hours of additional support during the week. Sofie is achieving expected levels in all subjects. Whilst she is academically able, she experiences difficulties with organisation and sequencing skills which can lead to confusion during whole-class lessons. This confusion increases Sofie's anxieties which may then prevent her from engaging in the lesson.

Following lesson organisation and coping with change

Sofie uses a written work system, provided in a notebook, which identifies the sequence of activities in each lesson to help her follow the lesson organisation. The written work system for class lessons is entered into the notebook by the class teacher or the support assistant each afternoon for the following day's lessons so that they are available at the start of lessons. Sofie follows the written list of lesson activities, marking off each activity

---

Literacy lessons: imperative verbs

☐ Whole class: listen and watch the smartboard

☐ Work in book: 'Eyes on Danish' ~~page 21~~ page 38
>   *Need help?: raise your hand and wait for Søren to join you*

☐ Quiz & exchange: imperative verbs

REMEMBER: Imperative verbs are also known as 'bossy' verbs because they tell you what to do. We put imperative verbs at the beginning of a sentence, which automatically changes them into commands or actions that must be done.

1. Choose an imperative verb with Søren
2. Walk around class until Søren says: *(Find a partner)*
3. Find your partner
4. **First** read your word aloud – your partner should then act upon your instruction
5. **Then** listen as your partner read his/her word – you act upon the word
6. Start again at number 1. Continue until the timer bell rings, then the lesson is finished.

☐ Whole class: Emma passes chocolate coated marsmallow treats to the class

Figure 6.12 Work system with visual instructions for whole-class lesson.

as it is completed. Written instructions are added next to lesson activities to provide details about what is required at each stage of the lesson. This system provides Sofie with clear expectations and helps her to understand the organisation and sequence of the lesson.

Sofie quickly learned to use this written system independently, although still found it difficult when any changes are made to the lesson. To address this, the class teacher now writes any changes to the lesson on the class whiteboard and Sofie has been taught to amend her work system by crossing out the 'old' information and writing in the new information (see Figure 6.12).

This system enables Sofie to develop organisation and sequencing skills and to cope with managing changes to lessons across the curriculum. These are key skills which are important to develop as curriculum access depends in part upon learners feeling confident and understanding the organisation of lessons. If, as in Sofie's case, learners are anxious about concepts such as 'what work, how much work, in what order, what to do with finished and unfinished work', this creates barriers to accessing curriculum content as the learner over-focuses upon lesson organisation and not lesson content. These barriers are exacerbated during whole-class lessons when learners are to work as partners or in groups. By teaching learners strategies which help them to follow lesson organisation, this enables them to focus on developing the knowledge, understanding and skills which are being taught during lessons. For learners like Sofie who are able to process written information effectively, and who have or are developing useful skills in using technology, it is then possible to integrate written systems into electronic organisers.

Using work systems in secondary mainstream settings

Developing skills through work-related learning

Work systems are flexible and should be designed to meet individual learning needs. For learners included in mainstream secondary schools, the work system can be a helpful strategy both for classroom-based learning and also for learning within the community, for example during work experience. Work systems that are part of a schedule may be helpful to some and may be used within folders or personal organisers on smartphones or tablets. These can be adapted to be used in a wide range of contexts. The use of a work system is not confined to individuals with ASD; indeed many of us use work systems in our everyday lives by writing lists and crossing off completed tasks, often with great satisfaction! The difference is that most of us can set up and implement our own system, while people with ASD need help with each part of the process. The use of the work system is one strategy that can help prepare learners with ASD for life beyond school, within college and workplace contexts. Learners should be engaged in 'learning for work' by continuing to develop key skills through opportunities for 'work-related learning'. For those with ASD this will require structured approaches to enable them to participate in work-related learning and to learn how to organise themselves in the workplace. The following example illustrates the use of a work system in school and during work experience.

Case study

Written work system embedded in the schedule

Adam is 15 years old and attends a local mainstream secondary school where he is studying for his examinations. Adam uses a student planner that incorporates a written daily schedule (Chapter 5). The schedule also includes his work system combining a written and number system (Figure 6.13). Adam prepares this with a LSA each morning at the learning support base.

Adam uses his work system for independent work and lessons in the mainstream school. He has daily opportunities for working independently within the learning support base to consolidate learned skills and to develop his concentration and attention span for lengthier periods. During these work sessions, Adam uses a series of labelled 'in' and 'out' office trays that contain labelled tasks, corresponding to the tasks indicated on his schedule for that particular lesson. During lessons in mainstream classrooms, Adam has learned to construct his work system by writing the teacher's verbal instructions onto his schedule in the appropriate place. In addition, he has labelled plastic zip wallets in his file to keep additional instructions that have been prepared by learning support staff and equipment for particular lessons (Chapter 7). His work system reminds him when he needs to use these items. Adam's work system sometimes incorporates questions to remind him to check he has everything he needs.

Adam also uses a work system to organise his homework; this is prepared with his teacher or LSA in the learning support department. He uses his work system to overcome organisational difficulties and to ensure that he has essential resources for lessons. It also helps him to complete homework and to know who to hand it in to and when.

As Adam has learned to take increasing responsibility for organising his time and work, he is now being encouraged to use his smartphone to organise his daily schedule and incorporate tasks and instructions for each lesson with the support of a LSA. The school's VLE includes an area where teachers can post messages and reminders for individual learners; for Adam, this is set up to allow him to access important information about homework.

Work experience

The work system was also used when Adam went to a local library for work experience. Adam's schedule was prepared with support from a mentor identified in the workplace.

Monday	Week A
8.30 a.m.	Learning support: check schedule for the day
8.45 a.m.	English 101 (LSA: Mrs Smith) **(English wallet)**
	<u>Poetry composition</u>
	listen
	write poem
	show Mr Wall
10.30 a.m.	Break: library or outside
11.00 a.m.	Maths 205 (LSA: Mrs Taylor) **(maths wallet)**
	<u>Fractions</u>
	listen
	worksheet 3
	homework – worksheet 4
11.45 a.m.	Learning support – independent study time 3a 6b 2a break
12.15 p.m.	Lunch break: outside or learning support
1.30 p.m.	PE: field (what equipment?)
3.00 p.m.	Learning support: check homework diary and schedule for tomorrow
Reminders:	
raise my hand rather than interrupt	
work that is not finished can be filed as unfinished – check with the tutor when to finish it	

Figure 6.13 Work system incorporated on schedule.

```
Thursday 17th May

8.30 a.m.    Library
             Job: stock replacement (tell Miss Thorpe when finished)
10.15 a.m.   Break   Make coffee   read magazine
10.45 a.m.   Job: returns desk
12.00 noon   Lunch break
1.00 p.m.    Job: photocopying (tell Mrs Green when finished)
2.45 p.m.    Break
3.00 p.m.    Job: tidy store (tell Miss Thorpe when finished)
4.00 p.m.    Home


Reminder:
when I need help, ask Miss Thorpe
```

Figure 6.14 Work system on schedule used for work experience.

Each morning, Adam's work system was incorporated onto his schedule with help from the mentor (Figure 6.14). This enabled Adam to know what jobs he had to complete, in what order and when breaks would occur. Further visual instructions were available to help him to complete each job and to structure his break times (Chapter 7).

By the end of the work experience, Adam was able to complete all allocated jobs independently and was described as a conscientious and reliable worker.

Adam's combined schedule and work system is used to help him to become as independent as possible, both in school and in other settings. In addition, Adam is provided with opportunities for making choices and decisions, within both the schedule and the work system. The structure that Adam has learnt to use is transferable to contexts outside school and will be useful for him in adulthood.

Conclusion

Work systems are an essential part of Structured Teaching that enable learners to become organised, to concentrate, stay engaged and to complete tasks set. They can be an effective strategy for responding to the particular learning styles of individuals with ASD by providing clear visual cues and organisation. Within a work system, learners who are ready can be provided with opportunities for communication and making choices and decisions. Work systems are individualised to help to improve curriculum access and facilitate inclusion in different curriculum areas (Table 6.1).

As with the other elements of structure, assessment of developmental and cognitive abilities will be critical in establishing which type of work system will be helpful for an individual pupil. The aim for the individual is to provide a system that is most functional and leads to greatest independence for him. This will require individual target setting and careful monitoring and reviewing to ensure that the work system is effective. An individualised work system provides a structured organisational framework that should enable learners to participate.

Schedules and work systems are helpful in that they provide learners with important information, in a form that they best understand, about the sequence of events during the day and about how to get organised. If the schedule and work system are appropriate to the individual needs of the learner, he will know what is going to happen, when and where. He will also know how much work he has to do,

Table 6.1 Access to the curriculum through use of work systems

Early Years	Work systems promote: independence in carrying out activities; independent use of resources; concentration and focus.
Key skills across the curriculum	Work systems promote: communication about what to do; organisational skills; everyday problem solving. Work systems can also support working with others.
Personal and social education	Work systems help learners to: manage own behaviour and develop self-control; develop personal autonomy; make choices; take responsibility and feel positive about themselves and what they can achieve.
Wider curriculum	Work systems can be used to support the wider curriculum, for example vocational/work-related learning.

where to get it from, how he is progressing, what to do with the work when he has finished and what he should do next. This does not however complete the picture. The learner may understand from his schedule that it is time for the numeracy lesson and he may find the work he has to do; however, when he looks at the task he may be unsure as to how to complete it. Additional visual information is needed so that learners know how to complete an activity or task. Chapter 7 provides examples that illustrate how additional visual information helps learners with understanding and completing a variety of tasks, with examples from varied curriculum subjects.

Chapter 7

Visual information
Adding meaning

Overview

Visual structure can be used to organise, clarify and differentiate tasks and assignments. It provides learners with information about what is expected, how to complete a task and how to use the required materials. Because visual skills are often especially strong in autism, and generally stronger than receptive language skills, visual information can be very helpful in developing understanding and helping learners to carry out class assignments. If learners are taught to look for visual information in all of their activities, they can use this information to understand and perform their work more effectively. Three kinds of visual information are important: visual clarity, visual organisation and visual instructions.

Visual clarity draws or engages the learner's attention to important or relevant information. It is a way of explaining and directing the person with ASD to the aspects of the task that are most central. Colour-coding and highlighting are the two most common ways of utilising visual clarity.

Visual organisation involves the way that space and containers are used to organise tasks or assignments. The organisation can convey a sense of orderliness that is very helpful for people with ASD. The organisation of a task can also limit the focus of their attention and make it easier for them to identify and stay attentive to the most relevant information. Organising containers, limiting materials and dividing and stabilising tasks are effective ways to utilise visual organisation. These organisational strategies allow learners to focus on their tasks instead of endlessly, and usually unsuccessfully, organising their materials.

Visual instructions are written or pictorial cues that provide information about how to do an assignment or put the distinct parts of a task together correctly. They can include written instructions, pictured instructions with words, jigs, or product samples (actual prototypes of what you want the learner to make). Learners who consistently use visual instructions are much more flexible because the instructions can always be changed when the task demands need to be altered. The rigidity that sometimes characterises learners with ASD is reduced when they become engaged in following such instructions, rather than always doing tasks in their own idiosyncratic way. The basis for this greater flexibility, for learners and teachers, is because instructions can be varied depending upon the approach or outcome required; the individual is learning to follow the instructions as the routine and these instructions can be altered to increase flexibility and to encourage simple problem solving.

Using additional visual information as a strategy for differentiation

The principles for inclusion in any curriculum means that teachers should respond to learning needs and overcome potential barriers to learning. The predominantly visual learning style of many learners with ASD means that in order to address these principles it is essential to provide additional visual information that will add meaning to specific tasks and activities. Useful examples illustrate how teachers can address these principles including for example: using teaching approaches appropriate to different learning styles; using visual and written materials in different formats, including print, symbols and text; using alternative and augmentative communication, including signs and symbols; using ICT, visual and other materials to increase learners' knowledge of the wider world. The use of visual information provides a useful strategy for increasing understanding of specific tasks and activities and can be an effective way of differentiating tasks for learners with ASD.

Improving the physical structure and introducing schedules and work systems are helpful elements of Structured Teaching that enable learners to make more sense of what is expected of them. These strategies can help learners to concentrate, to understand what will be happening and to develop independent organisational skills; as such, these strategies are helpful in developing an effective learning environment for learners with ASD. However, in addition to creating an effective learning environment, learners will need further visual information to increase their understanding of a lesson and what they need to do in order to complete tasks. For example, the schedule tells the learner it is time for numeracy, a work system is used to enable the learner to organise his work and additional visual information increases the learner's understanding of the task itself.

Elements of visual information can help to add meaning to tasks and activities, both subject-based and in relation to other aspects of the curriculum, for example assemblies and playtimes. The purpose of this chapter is to provide examples that illustrate how the use of visual information can enhance meaning in a range of lessons and activities. Differentiation of tasks using visual information is individualised according to cognitive and developmental abilities, hence the examples provided may not be automatically transferable to other learners. Examples are provided to illustrate the principles of using the additional visual information that teachers and support staff will need in order to adapt and differentiate tasks, based on an assessment of individual learning needs. Learners will need to be taught to look for visual information to help them to understand concepts presented during a lesson, what is required to complete tasks and how to begin to problem solve.

Visual information can be used to add meaning to tasks and activities in a number of different contexts and for a variety of reasons:

- independent practising and consolidating skills that have previously been taught;
- independent work times;
- increasing meaning of tasks within group and whole-class lessons;
- developing problem-solving and investigative skills;
- developing independence in everyday routines.

Visual information is a useful strategy for differentiating planning and teaching in all curriculum subjects and can also be used to help learners to develop key skills and thinking skills. The following examples illustrate ways in which visual information can be used to differentiate for learners with ASD.

Introducing additional visual information

The elements of visual structure for differentiating tasks include the need to consider visual clarity, visual organisation of tasks and visual instructions. For learners in the early years and for learners with severe learning difficulties, tasks can be visually structured to ensure that the concept or purpose of the task is clarified. Visual organisation of the task materials can also help to increase understanding of what is required. For many learners with ASD the organisation of task materials will be important. Just as learners may have difficulties with organising themselves in relation to where to get their work from and where to put it when it is finished, equally they have difficulties with organising the materials within a task. Whilst the work system helps the learner to find his work and to put it away when it is finished, additional visual information is then required to help him to organise the task materials. Sometimes learners will not complete tasks due to confusion or anxiety relating to the materials. For example, items for sorting that fall onto the floor may cause distress and the learner may then not complete the task. Organisation of materials into containers that are fixed may alleviate this anxiety and enable the learner to complete the task. At this level, additional visual instructions are not used; the task is visually clarified and organised to ensure that the learner will not require any further instructions. The use of 'shoebox tasks' have become a popular way of visually structuring tasks to provide clarity and organisation of task materials which enables independence.

Case study

Introducing structured tasks

Sam is three years old and attends an integrated nursery. He is learning to use transition objects to move between activities in the nursery and is being taught how to use a basic work system with a 'finished' box to develop organisational skills. Sam is frequently overwhelmed when presented with too many materials and will often throw them onto the floor. During one-to-one teaching times, Sam is working towards early learning goals in relation to communication, language and literacy and mathematical development. He is presented with tasks that have been visually structured to clarify and enhance the meaning of what he is to do. Materials are organised into fixed containers so that he does not lose resources and each task is presented within a shoebox or tray to reduce the need for Sam to organise materials. Tasks are organised in a left to right or top to bottom sequence, hence all the materials are organised in containers on the left, or at the top, within the shoebox or tray. Sam is taught to follow left to right and top to bottom organisational routines as the first step to independence in completing tasks. As Sam learns to complete each task during one-to-one teaching, tasks are transferred to independent work which he completes in a work-bay with no distractions; this enables Sam to continue to practice learned skills.

The following examples illustrate tasks that have been visually structured to help Sam to develop basic skills within the Early Years curriculum. Resources have been chosen that are interesting and motivating to Sam.

Mathematical development: shapes

Sam is particularly interested in textures and shapes and is learning to match a range of materials through the use of visually structured tasks. The following task is completed with adult support (Figure 7.1).

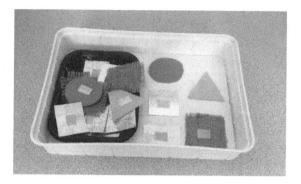

Figure 7.1 Independent task: mathematical development.

The shapes in this task are made of different fabrics as Sam likes to feel different textures so this interest helps him to make the correct match. Materials are organised left to right and Velcro is used to ensure the materials stay in place once matched. Sam does not have to organise any materials and can therefore concentrate on the task concepts. Similarly materials can be presented within a structured shoebox to help Sam to clearly see what he is supposed to do and to help reduce frustrations that may arise due to poor organisational skills. For example, later Sam will be taught to match and sort shapes without the texture cues (Figure 7.2). Introducing different shapes for Sam to sort varies the task and helps him to make progress. The visual organisation of the task helps Sam to focus on the sorting concept, rather than worry about organising the materials.

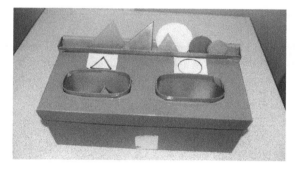

Figure 7.2 Developing independence: mathematical development.

Hand–eye coordination

Sam is also using play materials to work towards individual targets in relation to early learning goals. The following example illustrates how a stacking toy is organised to help Sam to practise hand–eye coordination (Figure 7.3). Again, this task has been organised for Sam to take the shapes from the left, working top to bottom, in order to complete stacking. Without the visual organisation of the resources, Sam would quickly become disorganised and confused as to what to do and would probably abandon the activity.

Figure 7.3 Independent task: hand–eye coordination.

Visual organisation enables Sam to understand how to complete activities; he still needs support at this stage but will become increasingly independent as he makes progress. Sam's activities and tasks are often visually structured by nursery assistants after working with the teacher during the planning stage. For example, the left to right and/ or top to bottom organisation of materials can be used in a wide range of activities including cooking, water play and so on.

Sam is currently learning to complete activities with support. Once he has learnt to complete a task he will be taught to practise his new skill during an independent work time, using his work system. This will provide Sam with opportunities to rehearse and consolidate new skills independently. As he learns new skills, these can be transferred to independent work time and he can continue to learn new skills within his one-to-one teaching times. Ongoing monitoring, recording and reviewing of Sam's independent tasks will be important to ensure that Sam continues to make progress and does not become bored by too much repetition. While he needs some repetition at this stage, in order to consolidate his learning, it is important to also consider progress within the independent work time. Sam's independent work tasks are curriculum referenced to early learning goals and linked to individual targets; this enables Sam's teacher to closely monitor Sam's progress and to update independent tasks when appropriate.

Visual information can be helpful to clarify the purpose of activities and tasks focusing on the early learning goals. Older pupils with ASD and learning difficulties may also require this level of organisation and clarification to increase their understanding of task concepts.

Case study

Developing structured tasks

Martin is 14 and attends a special school. He is placed in a specialist class for six learners with ASD. Martin uses an object schedule and a left to right work system. Additional visual information is used to help Martin to complete a variety of tasks independently. Martin has independent work times scheduled daily in order to provide opportunities for him to consolidate new skills and to practise independent organisational and study skills. These independent study times are used for subject-based tasks that are curriculum referenced and for working towards individual targets. Visual information is also used during group and class lessons, for example for tasks within a science lesson. In addition, Martin is helped by additional visual information to take part in other activities, for example mini-enterprise. Martin is helped to understand how to complete specific tasks by visual clarification and organisation. Martin's tasks are presented in varying containers including shoeboxes, trays, baskets and folders to increase his flexibility. The following examples illustrate how visual information is used to help Martin to work in small groups and independently.

Science

Visual information is used to help Martin complete tasks during class lessons, for example, in a series of science lessons where learners are observing chemical reactions and mixtures. One of the lessons requires learners to pour red cabbage water onto a variety of everyday substances to observe and record the outcomes. Martin is helped to record the results by grouping items that change to the same colour (pink or blue) and taking a photograph of each group. A structured task is prepared for Martin and a peer, with support from adults to complete the task. The visual information for this task is shown in Figure 7.4.

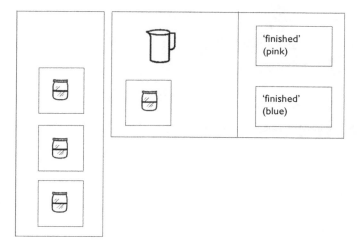

Figure 7.4 Visual organisation: science.

Martin and one peer follow the left to right organisation of the activity and materials to help them to test each item systematically. Coloured tape indicates how much cabbage water to pour into each container. The organisation of two 'finished' containers, coloured pink and blue, on the right also supports Martin and his peer to observe the colour reaction and to make a decision as to where to place the mixture. Without this visual information, the learners would become confused and this may lead to challenging behaviour. Visual information helps Martin to understand what he is to do and supports him in developing investigative skills. He still requires support from an adult during this lesson, but the adult can now spend her time helping to reinforce the lesson concept, rather than organising the materials for the learners. Through the use of visual structure, Martin is more likely to stay and participate in the lesson, achieving his targets in science to group objects and materials in terms of simple features or properties and to engage in experimentation with a range of equipment in familiar and relevant situations.

Speaking and listening

As part of his work in English, Martin is being encouraged to communicate with his family about events at school and also to communicate with his teacher about events at home. In addition, he is further encouraged to communicate this information to staff at the respite centre which he attends one weekend per month. Martin has a communication book in the form of a diary which is used for this purpose. With the use of visual information, Martin completes the diary each day, with support, using objects, or logos from packaging, to represent what he has done, what he enjoyed and so on (Figure 7.5). This diary is one example of the ways in which Martin and other learners are being provided with opportunities to be involved in making simple visual and/or tactile records which reflect their everyday experiences; recording events in this way also provides a visual tool to encourage Martin to develop his episodic memory.

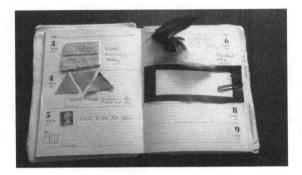

Figure 7.5 Visual clarity: communication.

This activity is supported by an adult, within a routine structure. The task is visually organised to follow a left to right organisation of resources. Objects and logos for specific places or events are collected during the day and placed in a container (on the left) for Martin to select. The correct day in the diary is highlighted for Martin to record the chosen event(s). The supporting adult talks about Martin's choice with him and writes a comment if appropriate. As Martin learns to recognise pictures, the communication book can continue using pictures. Thus Martin is using objects and logos to communicate information to others.

Mini-enterprise

Visual information is equally important outside the classroom. Martin's year group has taken part in a mini-enterprise project involving cleaning cars and mini-buses as part of their work in relation to enterprise and entrepreneurial skills. Martin learned to wash wheels, lights and registration plates as part of the project. This required visual information and organisation to help Martin to complete his tasks independently. Washing materials were provided in one bucket and rinsing water and cloth in a second. These were arranged to follow in a left to right sequence and also taught as a 'first ... then...' routine, 'first wash, then rinse'. Coloured stickers were used to indicate which areas Martin should clean. Martin was taught to begin at the left and work his way round the vehicle looking for stickers. A 'finished' bucket was used by all learners for materials they had used and were finished with.

Independent tasks: numeracy

This activity also led to developing individual tasks for Martin that would enable him to practise and consolidate basic skills. For example, after collecting payment for cleaning cars, Martin sorted coins into moneybags in order to take them to the bank (Figure 7.6). This task allows Martin to reinforce his ability to recognise coins within a meaningful, real-life context linked to the mini-enterprise project. The materials are organised in a tray for Martin to work from left to right. Coloured tape clarifies where to open individual moneybags.

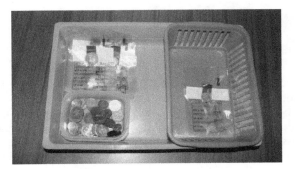

Figure 7.6 Independent numeracy task, linked to mini-enterprise project.

Visual information for Martin focuses upon visual organisation and clarity, rather than extra visual instructions that he will not yet understand. Some learners will be able to follow simple, to complex, visual instructions that help them to understand and access lessons. The following examples illustrate the use of picture/word instructions for independent work, group work and playtimes.

Case study

Picture instructions

Some pupils understand pictures and photographs and can follow picture instructions. Ricky is six years old, has ASD and learning difficulties and attends specialist autism provision within a school for children with a range of special educational needs. He uses a photograph schedule (Chapter 3) and a colour/shape matching work system (Chapter 6). Additional visual information is used to help Ricky to work independently and to follow visual instructions in group and class lessons. Ricky has daily independent work times for practising learnt skills and to reinforce specific concepts. He completes tasks relating to core subjects on a daily basis. In addition, topic-related tasks are structured for core subjects and for activities such as structured play.

Literacy

During independent work time in the literacy hour, Ricky completes tasks that are designed to provide him with opportunities to consolidate learnt skills linked to the literacy lesson or to individual targets. For example, following a school trip to a local farm park, and a subsequent lesson based upon a story about farm animals, Ricky works independently matching pictures of farm animals that appear in the story (Figure 7.7).

Figure 7.7 Independent task: literacy.

This task is organised in a left to right sequence for Ricky within a folder. He has been taught to match the photos following the top to bottom sequence on each page. The left to right and top to bottom routines reinforce reading direction and the task also reinforces Ricky's knowledge of how books work. As Ricky begins to recognise symbols, the task can progress to matching symbols to photographs. Further progress may lead to a similar structured activity to help Ricky to construct his own story about farm animals with adult support, with a selection of coloured pictures to choose from and a prepared template on which Ricky can place his pictures (Figure 7.8). The adult can then discuss appropriate captions with him, later he may write his own caption using symbols. The task is organised for Ricky and the use of Velcro ensures that his materials stay in place once selected. Thus Ricky is provided with opportunities in literacy to write about events in personal experience within a structured activity and using familiar resources.

Figure 7.8 Visual structure: story composition.

Although Ricky is not yet writing the story himself, he is being supported to make a book using pictures and to offer suggestions for what to write. The visual template helps Ricky to organise himself to construct the book as independently as possible. This can be extended by providing different visual templates for the book layout from which Ricky can choose. Alternatively, as Ricky makes progress, ICT software may be used to set up story templates which Ricky can use with the same visual structure to enable independence.

Design and technology

Similar levels of visual information are used for other subject-based lessons. For example in design and technology, Ricky is learning to assemble, join and combine materials and components. Visual information is provided as picture instructions for Ricky to follow (Figure 7.9); without these visual instructions, Ricky loses interest or assembles materials in repetitive ways.

Figure 7.9 Picture instructions: assembling, joining and combining materials and components.

This activity is visually organised from left to right with a picture instruction for Ricky to follow. Ricky can be encouraged to become more flexible in his use of different components by following different picture instructions. For some learners it is possible

Figure 7.10 Visual instructions: early problem solving and thinking skills.

to incorporate elements of choice within the picture instructions, for example by omitting the colour of some components so that the learner still has instructions for the model but must decide on some of the colours. Similarly, by adding question marks the learner must decide which components to use for parts of the model. In this way, individuals can be encouraged to solve simple problems and develop early thinking skills within the security of the visual structure that has been provided (Figure 7.10).

Once Ricky can follow visual instructions, he can be encouraged to play alongside others. For example, picture instructions for assembling a variety of resources can be made available in the play area with the appropriate materials. Ricky is taught to play alongside another learner, with shared materials but following his own visual instructions.

Art and design

Visual information can also be incorporated into class lessons such as art. Ricky's class spent some time investigating patterns and the use of black and white. A variety of 'greyscale' visual images provided visual directions for producing patterns (for example see Figure 7.11).

Figure 7.11 Visual information: art.

The children were encouraged to choose an image that they could then use as a guide for their work. Without the visual directions, most of the learners would have daubed paint repetitively and not had the opportunity to produce patterns. Following the use of the directions, some began to produce their own patterns.

Playtimes

Visual information is equally important at other times. During playtimes Ricky follows a photograph work system to indicate which activities to complete. Without the use of the work system, Ricky wanders aimlessly and does not initiate nor engage in any activities. Although he likes to wander, if left for too long he will become distressed and frustrated. By providing a work system he can be guided to a range of activities, including a time for wandering. These instructions are followed top to bottom; Ricky follows the instructions, removing each photograph when it is time to finish the activity (indicated by a lunchtime supervisor ringing a bell). A typical break time might include a sequence such as 'bike, basketball, walk'. Further visual information helps Ricky to participate in the activities. For example, a 'road layout' on the playground clarifies where to ride his bike (without this he rides his bike over the field, which is designated for football). When Ricky joins the basketball activity a list of tokens are stuck on the wall, indicating how many turns he will have. In addition, a 'your turn' picture card is given to each learner when it is their turn. As Ricky has a turn, he places a token in a bucket; when all the tokens are gone from the wall and are in the 'finished' bucket, Ricky knows his turn is over. As Ricky becomes more familiar and confident with a range of activities, the instructions can be developed to include an element of choice. In this way, visual instructions are providing Ricky with opportunities to encourage him to begin to make simple choices. Playtimes can be opportune times for individuals to learn the key skill of 'working with others' within a structured play context. Visual information can help learners to understand what to do and reduces confusion, important precursors to learning to play alongside and with others.

Additional visual information is provided for learners depending upon their level of visual cognition. Visual organisation and instructions are individualised and can provide flexible ways of providing structure for a wide range of activities. Some learners will also understand symbols or icons and their understanding can be greatly enhanced by this type of visual information which supplements verbal directions.

Case study

Symbol instructions

Leila is nine years old and has autism and learning difficulties. She attends specialist provision within a mainstream school. Leila uses a part-day symbol schedule and number-matching work system. Additional visual information clarifies important information within a task, helps Leila to organise tasks and provides symbol instructions to identify the sequence of steps she needs to take in order to complete a task. The following examples illustrate how visual information is presented to help Leila to increase her understanding in group and class lessons, to work independently and to understand the sequence and purpose of specific activities such as assembly.

Literacy

During literacy lessons Leila has symbol instructions to supplement the teacher's verbal directions. Symbols are also used when Leila is working with others. During a literacy lesson that focuses upon writing, Leila is asked to write a letter to her mum about a recent residential trip linked to writing and composition targets: sequence events and recount them in appropriate detail; put ideas into sentences; use a clear structure to organise writing. Leila works with another learner who has special educational needs and an adult. Both learners use a visually structured 'ideas sheet' to help them to recount events (Figure 7.12). Following this, the adult helps Leila to complete her letter by referring to her ideas sheet and inserting symbols and words on a prepared letter using the computer.

Science

In science, Leila's class completed a series of lessons on 'growing' including growing beans, observing the stages of growth, recognising the parts of the plant and that the roots grow in the dark while the green leaves need light. During one lesson, Leila worked with another learner planting beans into individual pots. Symbol instructions were used by both learners to help them complete the activity. The worksheet followed a top to bottom, numbered sequence and key points and teaching points were clarified

Write a letter to your mum about a school trip

ideas

1. How did you travel?

2. Where did you stay?

where   caravan   house   farm

3. Who went?

who?

4. What did you do?

what?   swimming   walking   riding

5. What did you like?

like

Figure 7.12 Symbols: generating ideas during literacy.

by highlighting. The use of these instructions allowed Leila and her peer to be independent in carrying out each stage of the task. Without the instructions, Leila would need an adult to spend time with her on sequencing the task and organisation, rather than on emphasising the teaching points.

In addition, prior to the lesson, Leila was allocated the task of giving out materials to pairs of children. A symbol list (Figure 7.13) enabled her to fulfil this task without becoming confused by the large number of materials to deal with. The list was used to collect sets of materials to then give out to her peers, one of Leila's individual targets relating to developing her social skills. The list reduced anxieties relating to organisation and means Leila can concentrate on the social target towards which she is working.

Give each pair of children	Jane Sally	Tim Sam	Mark Amy	Gita Alex	Tina Beth
 2 plant pots					
 a bag of compost					
 I scoop					
2 beans					

Figure 7.13 Symbol list: working with others and social skills.

Developing independence

Visual information can be used to help learners to develop independent working skills across the range of subjects. Tasks that are designed to be completed independently may relate to class lessons or to individual targets. Such tasks should be monitored and progress and achievement recorded to ensure that learners are offered opportunities to consolidate their learning but also make progress. Independent tasks will be structured taking into account organisation of resources, clarity of what is required and instructions to help learners understand what to do.

In order to reinforce the sequence of growing, the class sequenced pictures of the stages of growth. An adult structured an activity for Leila to complete independently (Figure 7.14). This task makes use of symbolic pictures that Leila can match following a left to right, top to bottom sequence. Numbers also help Leila to complete the sequence correctly. This task was one of several designed to consolidate Leila's understanding of the growth of green plants.

Similar tasks can be made for individuals to consolidate their learning in other areas. When Leila's class were looking at skeletons, the LSA made a task that Leila and others could complete independently to rehearse and reinforce their recognition of body parts in relation to the skeleton (Figure 7.15). The task is organised in a tray with prepared cut-out body parts; Velcro is used to ensure the pieces stay in place – this is important for ensuring that the work can be checked later. If Leila had been given the worksheet and had been required to cut out the body parts and stick them to the skeleton, she would have become disorganised and upset and would have needed considerable help.

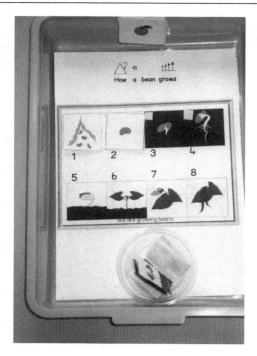

Figure 7.14 Independent task: science – green plants.

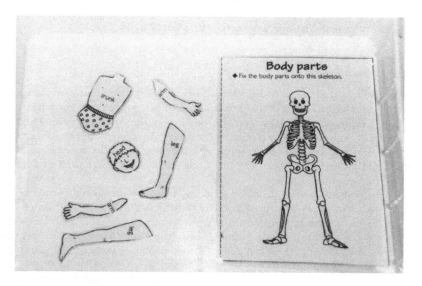

Figure 7.15 Independent task: science – the skeleton.

This would probably have distracted her from the relevant information relating to the task and she may well have focused entirely on organising materials rather than on the task objectives. This task allows Leila to complete the work independently without becoming distressed, enabling her to focus on matching body parts to the skeleton rather than on organising herself.

Physical education

Visual instructions can be incorporated into PE lessons for learners with ASD and other SEN. During a series of lessons focusing on movements and travelling Leila follows visual instructions (Figure 7.16) to help her to perform gymnastic activities with the following targets to: perform basic skills in travelling; develop the range of their skills and actions; choose and link skills and actions in short movement phrases.

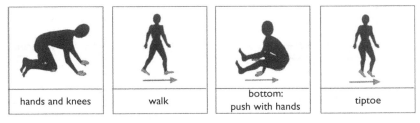

| hands and knees | walk | bottom: push with hands | tiptoe |

Figure 7.16 Visual instructions: PE.

Initially visual cues were used during a lesson using low-level apparatus arranged in a clear circuit. Visual cues were placed at each piece of apparatus to indicate how to travel, for example along a bench, and Leila was taught how to follow these instructions. As learners become familiar with the visual cues, they can be varied during the lesson and can be extended to encourage learners to follow a sequence of cues to link movements and/or to incorporate choice, encouraging creative thinking and imagination (Figure 7.17).

| tiptoe | what next? | skip |

Figure 7.17 Visual directions: choice and decision making – PE.

Encouraging early thinking skills across the curriculum

Visual information can also be used to encourage early thinking skills, such as remembering, across the curriculum. For example, Leila is developing personal autonomy in relation to making decisions in the community. Following a community visit, a support assistant discovered that Leila is unsure of which toilets she should use and frequently wandered into the 'gents'. Subsequently a series of community visits were set up to teach Leila to find the 'ladies' in a variety of contexts. The support assistant made a set of activities depicting the sequence of a variety of visits to encourage Leila to plan and also to decide which toilet symbol she should look for.

Figure 7.18 shows one such sequence (a selection of symbols is provided from which the learner may choose). This activity is completed with a support assistant and another learner before going on a visit into the community. Leila is encouraged to decide what

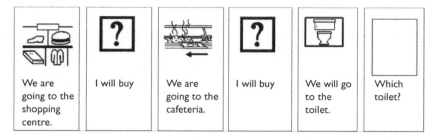

| We are going to the shopping centre. | I will buy | We are going to the cafeteria. | I will buy | We will go to the toilet. | Which toilet? |

Figure 7.18 Visual information to encourage early thinking skills and personal autonomy – PSHE.

she will buy and record her decision using a symbol. She then selects the symbol for the toilet she should use if she needs to during the community visit. The completed task is taken by Leila on her trip to remind her of her planning. The structure of this activity allows Leila to develop planning skills and to make decisions relating to everyday problems.

Other aspects of the curriculum

Visual cues also help Leila in a wide range of other ways. For example, during assemblies, she would become anxious about what would happen and often asked to leave part way through. Leila's teacher felt that Leila's anxiety was partly due to her lack of understanding about the organisation of assembly and when it would finish so that she could return to her classroom. Hence, an assembly book was provided for her to understand the sequence of assembly and when it would finish (Figure 7.19).

Figure 7.19 Visual cues: assembly book (one icon per page).

Leila was given a personal copy of the book, fastened with a treasury tag so that the sequence of events can be changed according to the assembly. A large version was also used for the whole school as it was felt that other children would also benefit from being able to follow this visual sequence. The person leading assembly orders the book according to their plan and a learner is selected at the beginning of each assembly to turn the pages as appropriate (Leila loves this job). This has now been extended to include the use of picture and symbol information to help learners to better understand the content of assembly.

Monitoring behaviour and following rules

Symbols are also used to visually remind Leila of appropriate behaviour in different lessons and contexts. For example, to remind Leila (and other learners) not to call out or interrupt, a symbol for 'hands up' is visible on the smart board at appropriate times during lessons (Figure 7.20).

The teacher finds this is a useful reminder that Leila is more likely to respond to, cutting down the need for constant verbal reminders that quickly become 'nagging'. This strategy is easily individualised for other pupils, for example by holding up a

hand up

Figure 7.20 Visual cue: reminder to raise hand rather than call out.

cut-out hand on a stick. Similar symbol cues can be used to remind learners about how they should be behaving or what they should be doing (Figure 7.21).

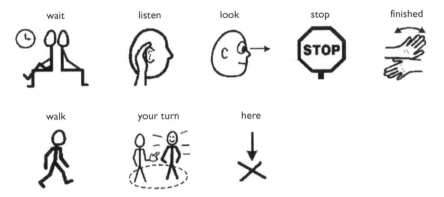

Figure 7.21 Examples of symbols used as visual reminders of appropriate behaviour.

Symbol cues visually remind learners of the important concepts during a lesson and are helpful when they become distracted. Individual symbols can be given to individual learners by support staff to remind them of expectations for behaviour. They can be used during lessons, at playtimes and lunchtimes, during assemblies and so on.

Visual information can be individualised to incorporate combinations of symbols and words for some learners. Different learners will require different levels of symbols depending upon their reading and comprehension ability. The following case study illustrates the use of a symbols and words by a group of learners to enable them to complete a vocational task.

Case study

Visual instructions to support cooperative vocational tasks

Kulpreet, Deepak, Ahmed and Sanjay are young adults aged 18–19 who attend a specialist educational setting for learners on the autism spectrum in India. They attend the educational setting daily and they participate in a variety of activities including vocational training. The vocational aspect of the curriculum is a priority, with the aim of preparing young adults to participate in work-related activities in the local community.

The students have a variety of skills which they use as part of independent tasks and which they are now learning to use as part of a cooperative work session. The physical structure, schedules and work system are essential components of structure which provide the students with: an effective learning environment; meaningful information about the sequence of activities during their day and who they will be working with; an organisational work system for working as part of a team. The final element of structure is the visual information the students need in order to make sense of their part of the task, to follow visual instructions and to encourage communication between them.

A sequence of simple instructions is posted on the screen in front of the students; these instructions combine symbols and words (see Figure 7.22).

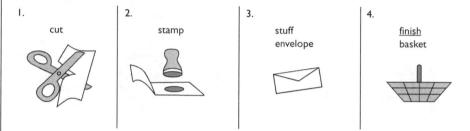

Figure 7.22 Vocational group-work instructions fixed on low level screen (see Figure 6.7).

Each student also follows visual cues and instructions to complete their task successfully:

1   Kulpreet's job is to take a sheet of paper from his work basket which includes letter or memo slips, the number of which vary depending upon the length of the letter or memo; each sheet typically includes three or four copies of each letter or memo. Kulpreet has good fine motor skills and can use scissors to cut along straight lines; a line of dashes mark where he is to cut and also indicate where to start cutting with a 'scissors' symbol.
2   Each letter or memo has an outline which clarifies for Deepak where he should add the school stamp (see Figure 7.23).
3   Ahmed uses a visual template showing him which way round to hold the envelope in which he places a slip (i.e. in such a way that the opening is facing upwards).
4   Supported by a TA, Sanjay delivers the post to the different departments in school.

It is important to note that in setting up this cooperative group work activity the students first needed to learn their part of the task. Each student was taught to use his visual cues and instructions in a one-to-one teaching session and then practised the task in independent work sessions each day. The group work activity was set up once each student had mastered their task independently; the students' tables were gradually moved closer to each other until they were adjacent. Once the activity was set up as group work, at first each student looked only at his own task; as they became more comfortable sitting next to each other, they began to look at each other and also at the task each student was completing. Each component of Structured Teaching required consideration in order to set up the cooperative group work activity; in addition, other strategies were drawn upon to enable the students to work together on a joint activity (see Chapter 9 for a full discussion of the blending of strategies for this example).

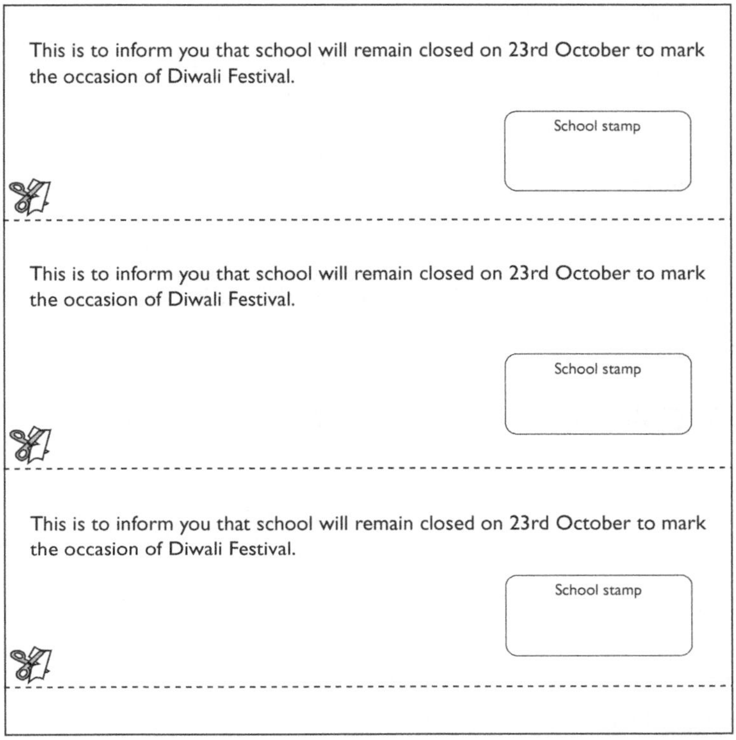

This is to inform you that school will remain closed on 23rd October to mark the occasion of Diwali Festival.

School stamp

This is to inform you that school will remain closed on 23rd October to mark the occasion of Diwali Festival.

School stamp

This is to inform you that school will remain closed on 23rd October to mark the occasion of Diwali Festival.

School stamp

Figure 7.23 Visual clarification to show where to 'cut' and 'stamp'.

Visual instructions may be presented to learners in a wide variety of ways. Developments in technology have resulted in many programmes and applications becoming available which may be particularly helpful to engage some learners. The following example illustrates how by presenting visual instructions using a tablet, which is motivating to the learner, this may encourage the learner to participate in a less-preferred activity.

Case study

Visual instructions provided on a tablet

Emily is 15 years old and attends a non-profit private elementary and secondary learning centre in North Carolina which meets the need of learners who need structure, consistency, positive reinforcement, more movement, reduced stress, both remediation and challenge along with a multi-sensory way of learning. Emily uses her structured systems independently and this helps her to focus upon lessons and activities.

Chapters 4, 5 and 6 illustrate how physical structure, schedule and a portable work system are important in supporting Emily to participate in food technology lessons and particularly in those which include preparation of food items which she dislikes. Whilst Emily is not easily distracted by her environment, she is often distracted by her 'worries'. In lessons which are likely to trigger her worries, such as a food technology lesson requiring handling of fruit, there is need to help her stay focused and engaged with the lesson. Visual instructions are therefore a crucial component of Emily's structure which supports her participation in the lesson by helping her to focus on the lesson rather than her worries.

Emily is highly motivated by technology, she loves using computers to search the Internet and she also likes to play computer games. This interest and preference for using technology is therefore utilised to support her to participate in a less-preferred activity, in this example a food technology lesson. For this reason, Emily's picture/written instructions for 'making a smoothie' are provided using a presentation programme on a tablet.

A picture/written list of ingredients is presented on one page of the presentation. The programme is animated so that as Emily collects each item, she touches the word on the ingredients list and a line appears, crossing out the item.

Figure 7.24 List of ingredients presented on tablet to encourage engagement.

Once all the ingredients have been gathered, one or two steps of the recipe instructions appear on a page. As Emily completes each step, she touches the word and it is crossed out. Touching the screen then turns the page to the next set of instructions. Figure 7.25 illustrates one page of the programme. Figure 7.25 shows the full set of instructions. Emily views one screen at a time, and touches each step when complete, which draws a line through that instruction.

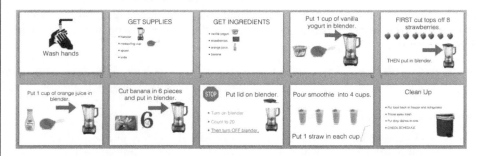

Figure 7.25 Screen shots of sequence of visual instructions.

In addition to using the programme on a tablet, other visual cues provide meaning and increase Emily's independence, including: colour-coded measuring cups which she fills to the top; cues to support counting ingredients, e.g. eight strawberries; a sign on the blender stating 'no licking'.

The use of a tablet increases Emily's engagement and independence and illustrates how, by using her interests to motivate her, she is able to participate in a lesson which she may have resisted due to her dislikes of the food items. Visual instruction and cues are helpful in providing access to a broad curriculum and are particularly effective in encouraging participation when strengths and interests are built into the structure.

The use of symbols can also enhance understanding for learners who are able to read written instructions. The following case study illustrates how David's understanding is supported with symbols to enable him to access a range of subject lessons.

Case study

Symbol/word instructions to access subject lessons

David attends a specialist school for learners with ASD. He is 11 years old and is preparing for transition to secondary provision with the support of an adult. David follows his symbol/word schedule independently and takes a portable version with him to the secondary school (Chapter 5). Additional visual directions help David to complete work independently, to increase his understanding during class lessons and to increase his independence in self-care areas. David follows simple written directions with symbols to supplement and increase his understanding and to encourage investigation and problem solving.

Science

David's class has been learning about electricity during their work on physical processes and David has joined in supported activities to learn how to complete simple circuits.

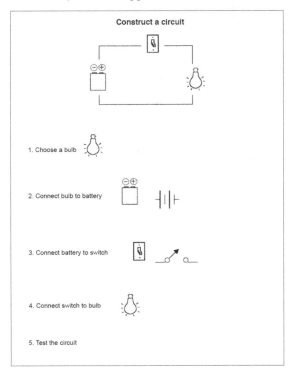

Figure 7.26 Visual instructions: science.

He can now construct circuits independently following written directions, with symbols to ensure understanding (Figure 7.26). Conventional symbols are placed alongside the symbols David is familiar with. Similar directions can be used to encourage him to investigate what happens when components in the circuit are changed, making bulbs brighter or dimmer, or to introduce buzzers or motors. Parts of the directions can be replaced with a '?' or a choice. By providing key visual information with elements of choice, or questions, David is encouraged to solve problems and investigate 'what happens if…?'

Independent tasks: mathematics

David has particular strengths in this curriculum subject and is able to be included in a mainstream class for mathematics lessons. Nevertheless, he still benefits from visual information to highlight, clarify and draw his attention to key points. For example, in a lesson focusing on ratio as part of the lesson learners are given a table to complete missing numbers using the ratio 1:2. David's worksheet has additional visual information to ensure that he focuses on the relevant concepts. David's interest in fast food and 'buy one get one free' offers is used to increase motivation (Figure 7.27). Key points and spaces for David's answers are highlighted for clarity and additional instructions remind him which operations he needs to use. A visual cue also reminds him to put up his hand if he needs help.

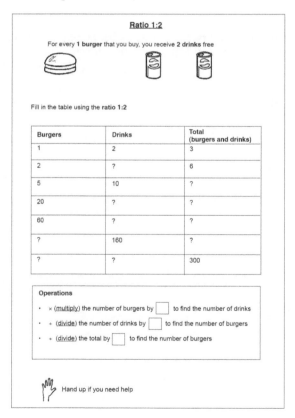

Figure 7.27 Clarifying and highlighting information on worksheets: numeracy.

Religious education

David's teacher adapted the scheme of work for RE for the class, following guidelines for teaching learners with learning difficulties. During a period of work based upon the Christian celebration of Easter, David's class visited a local church to find artefacts and pictures that link with the Easter story. David and his peers were provided with photographs to help focus their attention on relevant objects in the church. Without this visual information, David would have become distracted by the environment and would probably have forgotten what he was supposed to be looking for.

In addition, a symbol/word dictionary was prepared to help David and other pupils to develop their understanding of the key vocabulary used for the topic (Figure 7.28). This dictionary was referred to during a series of lessons to draw learners' attention to key concepts in the story. While David still has difficulties understanding the concepts of RE lessons, this example shows how visual information can help to increase meaning as far as possible.

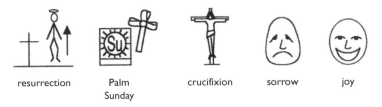

resurrection   Palm   crucifixion   sorrow   joy
                Sunday

Figure 7.28 Examples of symbols used in a symbol/word dictionary: RE.

Personal, social and health education

Despite his academic ability in some areas of the curriculum, David often becomes confused by everyday self-care tasks and as a result he has an individual target in the area of PSHE relating to personal hygiene. David was encouraged to follow symbol/word directions to complete routine self-care tasks because he had been observed trying to dress before he was dry and putting clothes on in an incorrect sequence and this caused him enormous distress. David also needed to learn to use deodorant appropriately. One of his half-termly targets was to follow visual directions in order to dry and dress himself and use deodorant in the correct sequence following swimming. Symbol/word directions were introduced following a top to bottom list (Figure 7.29). Some words do not need symbols as David can complete this step independently. The symbol for deodorant is larger than other symbols as this is a new step for David. The directions were put onto a laminated postcard that David kept in his swimming bag. He learnt to follow these directions and was able to use them with his parents when the family went swimming at weekends. David may eventually learn the routine of drying and dressing and may not need these directions in the future; however, some learners will need to keep directions such as these in order to maintain independence.

Figure 7.29 Symbol/word directions: PSHE – personal hygiene.

Some learners with ASD will be able to cope with written, and increasingly complex, instructions. Such may well respond to verbal directions, but this may result in dependence upon adults to provide verbal prompts. Written information reduces this dependence and increases the learner's autonomy. Written directions are also more meaningful to students with ASD so they lead to better learning and understanding.

Case study

Written instructions

Sarah is nine years old and has a diagnosis of ASD. She attends her local primary school and is supported by an adult during some lessons. Sarah has good expressive language, although this can mask her difficulties with comprehension. She has poor organisational and sequencing abilities and is unable to recall sequences of instructions. Sarah reads well and this strength has proven to be very useful in providing her with visual information. She follows written information, together with occasional symbols to help highlight or increase meaning when needed. The following examples illustrate how written information is used to help Sarah to work independently, to increase her understanding during class lessons and to remind her of social rules.

Literacy and ICT

In Chapter 6, Sarah's work system was illustrated to show how she can be more organised when working with peers during a literacy lesson, incorporating ICT. Sarah's class prepared a report for a school newsletter about their recent sports day; a 'jigsaw' approach was used to divide several tasks between groups (see Chapter 9 for examples of jigsaw planning combined with Structured Teaching) and Sarah's group was responsible for selecting and editing photographs, writing appropriate captions and reporting back to the whole class. Written instructions were prepared to remind Sarah how to use the ICT software to select and edit photographs and to add her captions (Figure 7.30).

These instructions were also used by other learners and were kept with a bank of similar ones that could be used in conjunction with a variety of ICT software. The instructions are laminated so that Sarah can use a dry-wipe pen to check off each instruction as she completes it. Note that Sarah is familiar with saving work and does not need instructions for where to save her file or what to call it; these instructions could be added for learners who need them. This example shows how written instructions help Sarah to develop thinking skills, for example information processing skills requiring learners to locate and collect relevant information.

Selecting and inserting photos
Writing captions

1. Open **Word**
2. Select **new page**
3. Click on **insert**
4. Click on **picture**
5. Click on **from file**
6. Click on the **C** drive
7. Click on the folder for **sports day**
8. Select the file you want to look at –
   double click on the name
9. Click on **text box**
10. **Draw** text box
11. Write **caption** for the photo

Repeat steps 3–11 to insert more photos

12. **Save** your work and **print**

Figure 7.30 Written instructions: ICT.

Visual information during whole-class teaching

During whole-class introductions to literacy, Sarah often has a prepared written vocabulary sheet to help her to focus on the relevant and important aspects of the lesson. For example, in sentence level work, Sarah's class was identifying adverbs with the suffix -ly and during one lesson the teacher showed the class some examples of classifying adverbs. Sarah's teacher and the support assistant discussed the lesson and the support assistant prepared a vocabulary sheet for Sarah to refer to during the whole-class discussion (Figure 7.31).

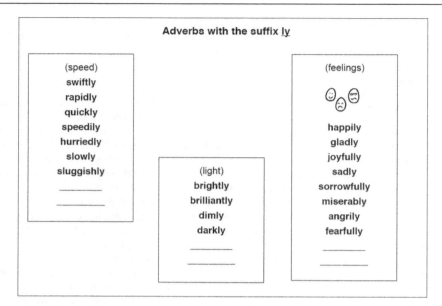

Figure 7.31 Written vocabulary sheet: literacy.

Having a prepared sheet helps Sarah to maintain her attention during the lesson. If she is distracted the support assistant can remind her to use her vocabulary sheet to regain her attention. Important elements of the information are highlighted to draw Sarah's attention, for example the suffix -ly is highlighted, the symbol for 'feelings' is used to increase meaning and spaces are left for Sarah to add any other words suggested during the lesson by her peers.

Finally, Sarah's teacher and the class support assistant always have highlighter pens in their pockets as one very quick way of drawing Sarah's attention to important and relevant information on worksheets is to highlight it. For example, 'small' words on a worksheet may be critical but may be missed by Sarah; highlighting words such as 'or', 'and' helps to draw Sarah's attention to the word and to then follow directions successfully. Highlighting also proved successful during shared reading when the teacher chose individual pupils to read aloud sections of text to the class. Sarah would become increasingly anxious about whether she would be chosen, and if chosen which section she would read. Consequently, she disrupted the reading with repetitive questions, she would not be able to listen to others reading and sometimes she would become distressed and have to leave the lesson. Sarah's teacher now highlights a section of text for Sarah if she is to be chosen. This way she knows in advance if she is to read aloud or not; she also knows which section she will read. This strategy of clarifying for Sarah the requirements of the activity reduced her anxiety and resulted in her being able to join in shared reading.

History

Learners who read instructions may also need additional symbols at times to increase meaning. Anxiety may result in the learner becoming 'de-skilled' in reading and understanding and in some instances this may be helped by adding symbols. Learners with ASD frequently have difficulties with some concepts; for example, understanding the past and concepts related to history can be particularly problematic. Sarah finds it difficult to distinguish events in the past from the present and certain historical topics cause her great anxiety. For example, when the class was learning about the Second World War Sarah became obsessive and afraid that she would have to be evacuated to live with a different family. While drawing upon relevant programmes of study to plan history schemes of work, Sarah's teacher also placed emphasis on 'the passage of time', drawing upon guidance for teaching learners with learning difficulties. Sarah's teacher developed with the class a written timeline for events in the recent, then increasingly distant, past to help Sarah and her peers to develop their sense of the passing of time (Figure 7.32).

1939–1944	1945	1952	1969	2000	2001 last year	Last month	Last week	Yester-day		Today
World War II	VE day (victory in Europe)	Corona-tion Queen Elizabeth II	Man landed on the moon	Millen-nium	'Harry Potter' film released	Queen's golden jubilee	Sports day	School party		School ends for summer

History   In the past   Finished

Here and now

Present

Figure 7.32 Visual timeline: history.

A timeline was hung from the classroom ceiling and as the class learned about new events they 'pegged' them onto the line in the appropriate place. Sarah kept her own laminated version so that she could update it on a daily basis. The distinction between past and present is highlighted and clarified, with an emphasis on events in the past being *finished*. Although Sarah still needs support from an adult during history lessons, she is becoming less anxious and confused about the distinction between past and present – a crucial first step in developing historical understanding.

Science

Written instructions are used by Sarah in a range of subject areas. These instructions clarify the task, but can also emphasise specific aspects that may be challenging such as 'investigating'.

During a science lesson on magnetism, Sarah follows written directions which supplement the teacher's verbal instructions. Scientific enquiry and investigation are crucial aspects of the lesson that may be challenging for Sarah.

Symbols are incorporated with her written directions to remind Sarah of what she needs to do in order to investigate, record and communicate her findings (Figure 7.33).

These symbols highlight important information for Sarah. In particular, the symbol for 'investigate' is highlighted and incorporates what Sarah needs to do. Similar strategies can be used to encourage learners to predict and research.

Visual instructions may remind learners of the steps they carried out to complete a task in order to record what they did. They may also help them to begin to sequence their own set of instructions as in the following example.

Design and technology: food technology

During a series of lessons, Sarah's class designed a set of menus to promote healthy eating, at the same time appealing to young children. The end of the project culminated in trying out their menus with children in an Early Years class, thus covering a number

 ▨▫▧▯▯ ✄ **1. <u>Choose</u> (4)**	paper wood stone metal ? ?
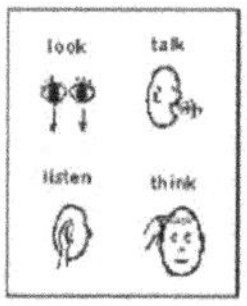 look talk 👀 🗣 listen think 👂 🧑 **2. <u>Investigate</u>**	Which materials are magnetic?
 ✋📄 **3. <u>Record</u>**	Put a <u>tick</u> next to the <u>magnetic materials</u>. Put a <u>cross</u> next to materials that are <u>not magnetic</u>.
 😊↔😊 **4. <u>Discuss</u>**	Bring your work to the group to talk about what you found out.

Figure 7.33 Visual instructions to encourage investigation.

of targets relating to developing, planning and communicating ideas, working with tools, equipment and materials and evaluating products. Sarah's group decided to plan a dessert using different fruits. Further directions helped Sarah and one peer to make their 'traffic light treat'. Sarah followed the written 'recipe' from top to bottom and used the smiley faces as a way of monitoring her progress through the sequence of steps (Figure 7.34).

Traffic light treat	
You need 1 kiwi fruit, 1 satsuma, 3 strawberries and some yoghurt.	😄
1. Peel a kiwi fruit, slice and put into the bottom of a glass.	😄
2. Peel the satsuma and place the segments on top of the kiwi fruit.	😄
3. Remove the stalk from the strawberries, wash them and slice them in half; place them on top of the satsuma segments.	
4. Spread the yoghurt on the top.	
5. Arrange 1 strawberry, 2 satsuma segments and 1 slice of kiwi fruit on the top to look like a traffic light.	

Figure 7.34 Written instructions: food technology.

As Sarah completes each step, she turns over the corresponding card on the right to reveal a smiley face. When the activity is finished, the board can be wiped clean and reused.

Sarah also used these instructions to help her to produce a similar set, with pictures, for the children in the Early Years class to make their own dessert. She decided to add a '?' to part of the instructions to encourage the children to choose one type of fruit, showing that her own awareness of making choices and simple decision making is developing.

Other aspects of the curriculum

Sarah's teacher uses written cue cards in a similar way to Leila's symbol cues. For example, Sarah does not realise that when the teacher talks to the whole class, she is also talking to Sarah. During whole-class teaching, Sarah's teacher places a written cue card (Figure 7.35) on her desk to remind Sarah that she should listen.

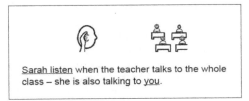

Sarah listen when the teacher talks to the whole class – she is also talking to you.

Figure 7.35 Written cue: listen during whole-class lessons.

Initially Sarah was handed her own personal cue card by the class support assistant; however the teacher found that by displaying the cue card at the front of the class, other children were also reminded to listen!

Written social rules

Written social rules are also used by Sarah's teacher to remind her about appropriate behaviour with peers. Sarah has a social rule written on her schedule reminding her to speak, not shout, when talking to peers (Figure 7.36).

Remember

Speak to other children in my group with a number 5 voice.

(1 = silence   **5 = speaking**   10 = shouting)

Figure 7.36 Written social rule.

The social rule is written onto Sarah's schedule as she is then provided with frequent opportunities to be reminded of it. This reduces 'verbal nagging' from adults and peers and when Sarah does shout, she is asked to read her rule on her schedule. Written directions such as these are important strategies to help learners with ASD to develop social skills which are important across the curriculum (see Chapter 9 for further examples of using visual instructions in combination with social scripts).

Like Sarah, other learners with ASD will be able to read written directions to help them to access different aspects of the curriculum. For some, written information will be critical in helping to reinforce understanding, reduce anxieties, increase organisational skills and improve communication with others. Others will be confident in reading instructions but may require further visual information to clarify important concepts and information and to enable the student to focus on relevant information. The following case study illustrates how visual clarification can be a useful differentiation strategy.

Case study

Adding visual cues and information for clarity and focus

Sofie is ten years old and attends a local mainstream school in a town in Denmark. She is currently in a class of 21 learners and she has five hours of additional support during the week. Sofie is achieving expected levels in all subjects. The use of a written work system and written instructions enable Sofie to independently follow the lesson organisation; for learners who are independent readers like Sofie, written instructions are an invaluable tool which can be used to support all curriculum subjects. However, the ability of fluent readers may sometimes mislead us into making assumptions about an individual's understanding of the most salient points within the text, for example on a worksheet or in a work book. This is the case for Sofie who, whilst a fluent reader, may focus on inappropriate detail in the text or may become visually overloaded by too much detail. The concept of providing visual clarity is an important one which is sometimes overlooked for the most academically able learners as we may assume that because they can read they will know and understand where to focus their attention. It is important in these circumstances to consider not only the need for written instructions, but also to consider how to visually clarify for the learners the detail which they need to focus on and/or the key concepts of the activity.

Whilst Sofie reads fluently and independently she sometimes finds it difficult to know where to focus her attention, particularly when presented with visually busy worksheets. Some simple strategies are considered when preparing work materials for Sofie and indeed these strategies are also helpful for other learners in the class. These strategies are used to highlight and clarify important information, drawing Sofie's attention to important information and enabling her to ignore irrelevant detail. For example, the teacher or support assistant may: number tasks on a worksheet to clarify the sequence in which tasks are to be completed; highlight key words, phrases, questions, and instructions to visually clarify where Sofie should focus her attention. Figure 6.12 illustrates how this is achieved in a literacy lesson. The reminder of the definition of imperative verbs is presented in bold and italics to draw Sofie's attention to important information whilst the speech bubble draws attention to an important action which Sofie needs to take.

Visual strategies such as these are not too time-consuming to provide, particularly when the learner's needs and visual strengths are identified and familiar to teachers and support staff. Such strategies enable learners like Sofie to focus their attention on important information which then enables them to demonstrate their knowledge and understanding.

The final case study demonstrates how the use of visual instructions can enhance access to the curriculum for learners who are academically able and who are taking increasing responsibility for their learning.

Case study

Further uses of written instructions

Adam is 15 years old and has Asperger Syndrome. He attends a local mainstream secondary school and is studying for important examinations. Adam uses a student planner that incorporates a written daily schedule and his work system (Chapter 5); he is also learning to use the school's VLE which he can access using a tablet. The teacher in charge of the learning support base found that Adam was helped significantly by visual cues and written information in relation to a number of areas. These were linked less to understanding lesson content, as Adam was generally able to understand and learn in most lessons. Visual information was sometimes used to help prepare Adam for lessons where content may be problematic, but more often for providing him with information to reduce his anxieties, about what to expect and how to behave.

Preparing for lessons

Adam goes to the learning support base regularly; a small group of learners have ASD and a specialist teacher teaches some of their lesson at the support base. The teacher is provided with advanced planning from Adam's subject teachers so that she can check to see if Adam will need any preparatory work before specific lessons. This pre-teaching may relate to lesson content or may be to prepare him for specific teaching approaches. The following example illustrates how visual information is provided to help Adam prepare for a geography lesson.

Geography

The theme of 'issues in physical geography' included some work on the Aswan High Dam as an example of a multi-purpose river scheme. Adam's class was to find out information relating to three questions and to prepare brief oral presentations for the next lesson. The teacher would introduce the lesson with key definitions, and then give all students envelopes containing information relating to the three questions about the River Nile flood and the dam. Adam would be working first in a pair to find out information relating to one of the questions, then joining to work collaboratively with another pair to explain and discuss what they have found out. The support teacher felt that Adam needed some visual information to help him to achieve the learning objectives which were to extract and summarise information from text, cartoons and diagrams and to work collaboratively in pairs and small groups. Visual information was used to highlight key points to listen for in the lesson and key vocabulary with written definitions was discussed. The teacher also discussed the main teaching and learning processes with Adam in order to prepare him for working collaboratively and to remind him of the rules when working with others (Figure 7.37). Adam placed this written information in the geography section of his file to refer to during the lesson; in addition, he could access this information which was also made available on the school's VLE.

Adam achieved the lesson objectives and worked with one peer successfully. Some adult support was still necessary to help him to collaborate as part of a small group – in

Geography Friday 8.45a.m.

The Aswan High Dam

- <u>Listen</u> for the explanation of '<u>multi-purpose scheme'</u> – write it down.
- Write down the 3 questions written on the board.
- Work with Jane – look at the information on the card together, check which question you have (1 or 2).
- Highlight information on the card that relates to the question.
- Summarise this information in bullet points.
- Join with Tim and Jon. Explain the important points relating to your question. <u>Listen</u> to Tim and Jon explain their points.
- <u>Listen</u> to the teacher give directions to the whole class, <u>write down the directions</u>.
- Work with Jane, Tim and Jon to prepare a presentation on '**what problems has the dam caused?**' Use the information on your cards to find out important points. The presentation should last <u>5 minutes</u>. <u>Remember to listen</u> to Jane, Tim and Jon and to <u>take turns in the conversation</u>.

Figure 7.37 Written directions: preparation for geography lesson.

this case the visual information also served as a reminder to the support assistant who could then provide Adam with consistent feedback and support.

Homework

Adam uses similar written directions to ensure that he understands homework requirements, completes homework on time and hands it in to the correct teacher. In order to clarify the importance of completing homework the support teacher provided a diagram that clarifies how much time needs to be spent on homework, in proportion to class lessons, when studying for examinations (Figure 7.38).

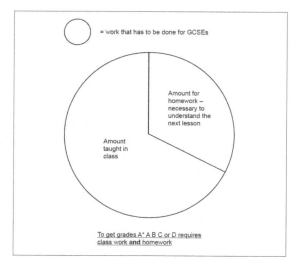

Figure 7.38 Visual information: homework requirements.

Reducing anxiety

Initially, when Adam joined the secondary school he spent the majority of his time in the learning support base. His teacher used visual information to help him to begin to enter classrooms around the school building. One of the first challenges to overcome was Adam's intense fear of entering a classroom. Adam's teacher found that if he had something visual upon which he could focus, he could then enter a classroom with less anxiety. A small blue dot was placed on the floor by his desk at the front of the class (see Figure 4.6) where he can see it from the classroom doorway. Adam was taught to focus on the dot and rehearsed entering classrooms with a support assistant. This enabled Adam to enter classrooms more easily. In addition, it was agreed that he should be able to leave a lesson if he became overly anxious and return to the learning support base. A written reminder was placed at the front of his student planner and also on the outside of his pencil case and a number line helped him to monitor his anxiety level (Figure 7.39). The written direction reduces his anxieties as it reminds Adam what he could do if he becomes stressed and how to do it politely. This strategy was communicated to all subject staff to ensure a consistent approach – most staff are happy to use the strategy as the alternative was that Adam would begin to shout and disrupt the lesson.

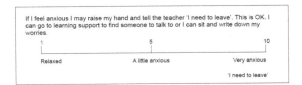

Figure 7.39 Written reminder: reducing anxiety.

Geography and citizenship posed further anxieties for Adam when he was asked to regularly watch world news in relation to 'sustainable development and economic issues in geography'. Prior to this, Adam had been discouraged from watching the news as he became overly distressed by world affairs that he could not control. The support teacher introduced Adam gradually to a children's news programme, before watching the main news, and taught him to write down main points of interest and any worries he might have as a result of a news item. A further strategy involved completing a table identifying Adam's main worries, who is responsible for dealing with the problem and what Adam and his family or friends could do in response to the news item. For example when Adam became anxious about poverty and famine in Ethiopia, written strategies helped him to consider the issues and to identify possible solutions and responses (Figure 7.40).

News item	Issues this raises that cause me to worry	Who is reponsible for helping and what might they do?	What I could do
• Famine in Ethiopia due to drought and failing crops – evening news	• People are hungry and may die of starvation • What if the crops fail again?	• Politicians in Ethiopia and Africa may arrange to receive food donations from other countries • Other countries and charities may arrange to send seed, equipment and advisers to help people in Africa to grow crops again	• Give a donation to a charity that is helping the victims • The charity shop will sell things I take and the charity use the money to send food, seed, machinery and/or advisers to Africa

Figure 7.40 Written information to reduce anxieties: geography and citizenship.

Written bullet points help Adam to communicate his concerns and also to identify strategies to deal with them. He has learnt to complete a table, following columns from left to right and filling in information as bullet points. Any blanks are then discussed with Adam and his support teacher and his family who help him to complete the table.

Written directions are also used to help Adam prepare for unfamiliar events. For example, he was invited to attend a sixth form presentation evening to help him decide which subjects he wished to study at advanced level. Adam was taught to communicate his worries and anxieties to his support teacher by email, and she would respond with an email as he found a written response more meaningful and helpful. Adam sent an email to the teacher listing his worries about the presentation evening as bullet points, including worries about what to wear, what time to arrive, who would be there, what would happen and when it would be appropriate to leave. Adam's teacher emailed a reply and provided him with a plan (Figure 7.41); this was also available via the VLE.

Written lists such as these are immensely helpful in supporting Adam with new events and activities. Important points can be highlighted and clarified by underlining, colour, bold and so on. Despite Adam's good academic performance, he still needs visual information to ensure that he can fully access all opportunities. Without the written list, Adam would probably not have attended the presentation evening.

- Do something relaxing (e.g. watch video, listen to music)

- Have dinner

- Change into appropriate **casual clothes**

- Ensure I have career's booklet with me before leaving in time to arrive at the school hall at **7.15p.m.**

- Sit in hall and use 'squeezy brain'

- The talk (given by Mr Taylor) willl begin at **7.30p.m.** and will last **approximately 30 minutes**

- Visit the various departments I am interested in. Walk and talk **calmly**

- Look at samples of work, talk to teachers and ask any questions I may have **(remember, wait for my turn)**

- Leave at approximately **9.15p.m. or before**

Figure 7.41 Visual instructions: preparation for sixth form presentation evening.

Extending visual information beyond school

Adam is a good example of a learner who will require visual information in different settings, particularly as his world expands and he moves away from the security of school. Preparation for entering work placements, college courses and further and higher education will require the same level of visual information if Adam is to feel confident and independent in increasingly demanding settings. Visual information was used during Adam's work experience in a library and the following example illustrates the importance of continuing the structure as Adam prepares for life beyond school.

Work-related learning

Adam completed work experience in a local library, as this was an environment that he felt comfortable in and where he would be able to use his skills. Adam used a schedule and work system (Chapters 5 and 6) and, in addition, further visual information was provided to help him to complete his jobs. The examples in Figure 7.42 illustrate instructions for replacing stock on the shelves and receiving returned books from customers.

Stock replacement

1. Find the book trolleys on the ground floor
2. Find the trolley with books 371–599
3. Take the trolley by lift to floor 2
4. Replace the books on the shelves using the classification numbers
5. Return to the ground floor and check schedule

Returns desk

1. Serve each customer one at a time – say good morning **or** good afternoon
2. Scan the bar code in each book
3. Check monitor to see if fee is due – tell customer the fee if they need to pay
4. Replace books on the trolley and say thank you to the customer

---

Figure 7.42 Written directions: work experience.

Similar instructions were used for jobs such as photocopying and tidying the store cupboard. Adam's instructions also indicated what to do during breaks, who to tell when finished and so on. A written list of 'conversation openers' was provided to help Adam initiate conversations with colleagues during break times. Adam completed the work experience very successfully, with one episode where he became anxious at having work checked. Written rules for who would check his work and how he should respond overcame this particular challenge.

Conclusion

Visual information is an essential component of Structured Teaching. It can help to clarify important concepts, provide organisation for how to tackle tasks and provide directions to help learners to complete their work. Visual information is also important because it is the best way to help students with ASD to learn and understand new information. Visual information is a useful differentiation strategy when planning and preparing work for learners with ASD. Clearly such information must be individualised; each learner will have different requirements as what helps one may not help another. This means it is impossible to provide structured lesson plans that can be copied for all other learners. The examples given in this chapter illustrate the principles of using visual information as a teaching style, in response to preferred learning styles and individual needs. Visual information is provided to help individual learners to understand what they are required to do and to increase the meaning of activities across the curriculum (Table 7.1).

As with all elements of Structured Teaching, visual information must be individualised for each learner. Ongoing monitoring of the use of this information is critical to ensure that the most appropriate information is provided to ensure that teaching and learning are meaningful for the individual. Visual information should be considered when planning lessons and activities for learners with ASD, for developing appropriate behaviour, to increase flexibility and to enable individuals to be included in all aspects of school and community life. The four elements of Structured Teaching, physical structure, schedules, work systems and visual information, together

Table 7.1 Access to the curriculum through use of visual information

Curriculum subjects	Differentiation of teaching strategies taking into account individual learning needs and preferred learning styles: visual clarification, organisation and instructions
Key skills	Visual information supports: communication; working with others; flexibility; making decisions; problem solving; information processing skills; enquiry skills
Wider curriculum	Visual information provides meaningful information to promote independence, self-reliance and autonomy across the whole curriculum, including vocational/work-related learning

provide essential strategies for learners with ASD. When each of these areas is considered, structure can be provided that overcomes barriers to learning and enables individuals to be included. While each element of Structured Teaching has been considered separately in this book, clearly if a learner with ASD is to benefit from similar structured strategies it is essential to consider all four elements in relation to the learner's individual needs (see Chapter 8). The resultant structure provides a framework within which a variety of other approaches and strategies can be combined; Chapter 9 provides examples of how to combine other approaches with Structured Teaching in order to promote access to the whole curriculum and to enhance wellbeing, learning and independence.

Tying it all together

This book has reviewed the fundamentals of Division TEACCH's Structured Teaching approach and how it can be used to help learners with ASD to access the curriculum. The authors have not taken any philosophical positions about whether any particular curriculum is useful or if it should be used with learners with ASD. Rather, the starting point for this presentation is that any subject curriculum exists as part of the whole curriculum to which all learners are entitled. The whole curriculum should provide breadth and balance, at the same time responding to individual learning needs. Structured Teaching provides some excellent strategies for helping learners with ASD to better access the curriculum, whatever that curriculum is; some of these productive strategies have been described in order to illustrate how the approach can facilitate curriculum access.

There are four essential components of Division TEACCH's Structured Teaching approach: physical structure, visual schedules, work systems and the visual structure of specific activities or tasks. Each of these parts of Structured Teaching helps learners with autism to access the curriculum in meaningful and important ways. In Chapter 4, physical structure is described and explained. For those with ASD, a clear, visually organised environment is the first step in making classrooms meaningful and manageable for them by creating a clear, predictable and autism-friendly environment, either in mainstream or specialised settings. For many of these learners, this will be their first step towards accessing the curriculum and is an important way of overcoming a major barrier to learning.

In addition to increasing understanding, the physical environment can also help reduce anxiety, which has a direct impact on a learner's behaviour and ability to learn. For example, the goals relating to personal, social and emotional development might include the need for learners to develop positive dispositions and attitudes, behaviour and self-control. These areas are often challenging for learners with ASD and are often priority areas of learning. A clear, consistent and predictable physical structure can promote these goals by reducing anxiety.

Working with others is identified as a key skill embedded in any curriculum and again is an area that can be challenging for learners with ASD. The physical space, and structure of that space, can be important in promoting the conditions that allow individuals with ASD to interact and work more effectively with others.

Organisation and study skills are additional key skills which present difficulties for learners with ASD. Clear boundaries that minimise distractions can help learners with ASD to develop the organisational and study skills that are needed to access all subjects across the curriculum. Teaching individuals to manage their own behaviour is another essential personal and social skill. The physical structure of the classroom can be a major factor in keeping learners with ASD calm, thus promoting self-management. Making meaningful choices is also influenced by a physical environment that makes choices clearer, and helps learners with ASD to understand what is available to them and when.

Physical structure can help learners to progress towards full participation in classroom activities. For example, defining areas with the use of small, portable screens or coloured tape can be useful in a wide variety of contexts. Screens, or visual demarcation, break up space, which is helpful for learners with ASD. These dividers can also clarify what is expected in certain areas and help individuals with ASD to concentrate.

In summary, effective physical structure of the classroom can promote goals relating to personal, social and emotional development. Physical structure can help learners to share space and work with others, develop organisation and study skills, personal and social skills and self-management of behaviour.

The second area of Structured Teaching, reviewed in Chapter 5, is visual schedules. These daily schedules provide visual information informing learners with ASD what will occur during their day and in what sequence. Visual schedules allow learners to anticipate and understand what will be happening to them and when. Schedules can be developed so that they are meaningful for learners with ASD at any level of functioning.

Daily schedules help learners with ASD to access the curriculum in a number of ways. The use of visual schedules can further curriculum goals by reducing confusion, and increasing flexibility, thereby encouraging access to a wider range of activities. Schedules also help increase curriculum access by: improving communication; improving understanding of what will happen, when and where; and improving transitions from lesson to lesson. Schedules are important because they can improve the general understanding of what goes on at school. Visual schedules also can be useful in redirecting students with ASD back to the activity they are supposed to be working on when they get distracted by other things occurring in the classroom.

Personal, social and emotional development are important elements of any curriculum and include developing a positive disposition to learn, as well as self-confidence and motivation. Schedules help promote these goals by teaching young children what is happening in their environment. The use of visual schedules and positive routines offers strategies for developing important skills identified in this area of learning.

Schedules can also help with transitions. They provide a consistent way for learners with ASD to change activities and a meaningful way for them to understand what is coming next. Schedules are very effective for facilitating these transitions and help learners in the early years to develop a positive approach to new experiences and to become confident to try new activities. They also help to prepare learners for changes that may occur in their routines. These areas may remain important goals for some learners throughout their education; schedules can be helpful in promoting these aspects of the curriculum at all ages and for all ability levels.

Communication and working with others are key skills necessary across any curriculum. In addition, learners with ASD will need support to develop early thinking skills such as recognising and obtaining information, predicting and anticipating, understanding cause and effect and linking objects, events and experiences. Structured Teaching's ways of using visual schedules help to address these areas. In particular, visual schedules help with social goals of working with others, listening and responding. For example, schedules enable learners to understand who the teacher is for a particular lesson, which facilitates attending to that person and participating in their lesson. Social situations can be anticipated by learners with autism and these appropriate expectations help their overall functioning in social and interpersonal situations.

Making choices and communicating preferences are crucial skills across the curriculum. Many learners with ASD have difficulties with the simplest of choices. Once secure in the use of a schedule, choices are more easily incorporated into their routine in order to understand and develop this choice-making skill.

Visual schedules, by allowing learners with ASD to function more independently in their environments, also facilitate access to aspects of personal, social and emotional curriculum goals and are helpful in teaching learners to manage and moderate their behaviour.

In summary, daily schedules can help in many important curriculum areas. They can facilitate the goals of personal, social and emotional development by promoting positive dispositions to learn, self-confidence and motivation. They also help to establish routines and prepare for change. Visual schedules help to promote key skills including communication, working with others and problem solving. These may include aspects such as recognising and obtaining information; predicting and anticipating; understanding cause and effect. Visual schedules also promote early thinking skills, such as learning to remember. Daily living skills, community skills, personal and social skills, and managing one's own behaviour are also promoted by the use of schedules. Finally, schedules can be helpful in promoting participation, making real choices and decisions, and meeting and working with others. Schedules can also facilitate work-related learning.

The third area of Structured Teaching, described in Chapter 6, is work systems. These are the systematic, individualised and meaningful strategies that are developed to help learners with ASD complete specific tasks. Individualised work systems help keep learners organised so that they can function independently and effectively in a variety of different activities. These systematic strategies can also be very effective in increasing access to different aspects of the curriculum. Work systems are critical for learners with ASD because they answer the four critical questions that are often unclear to them:

1 What work am I supposed to do?
2 How much work am I supposed to do?
3 How can I tell I am making progress and when will I be finished?
4 What will happen after I am finished?

Work systems are especially helpful in organising learners with ASD as they work on specific tasks in specific areas. For example, independent work systems are crucial for promoting aspects of personal, social and emotional development. These include independence in carrying out activities, attention, concentration and sitting quietly, independence within the environment, and independent use of resources. Learners should increase their confidence, try new activities, and attend, concentrate and sit quietly when appropriate. Work systems help young learners to work towards these goals and can be adapted for older learners who may need to continue to work towards these areas of learning as a priority.

Organisation and study skills are much more easily achieved through individual work systems. The work system is also an excellent strategy to help learners to fully participate in curricular activities by focusing on the learning environment, organisation and sequencing, motivation and concentration, and communication.

The need for learners to develop personal autonomy, to make meaningful choices and to communicate their choices applies across all curriculum subjects. Examples include increasing attention, interest, motivation, managing work time independently, completing tasks and taking responsibility for tasks by working independently. Access to the curriculum will be enhanced if learners are encouraged to develop these skills. These are major reasons why independent work systems were developed by Division TEACCH and these systems provide an excellent foundation for promoting these skills.

Although independent work systems are initially practised in independent work areas, they can also be used to encourage learners with ASD to interact with their classmates, thus encouraging learners to develop the key skill of working with others, which is required in all curriculum areas.

Curriculum goals include preparing learners to take responsibility, feel positive, develop personal autonomy and make choices. By promoting independent functioning and clarifying the concept of 'finished' so that learners feel a real sense of accomplishment, the work system can be instrumental in achieving these goals. The work system also facilitates generalisation by providing systematic strategies that learners can use in many different settings. Work system strategies can also be effective for work-related learning at older ages. Learners in secondary or high schools can be involved in work-related learning, which requires independent functioning, through the use of their work systems.

Work systems can also help learners to achieve the objective of being included in mainstream classrooms. Many learners with ASD can be successful in mainstream settings if they have these systematic, organised and visual strategies. By helping learners to overcome difficulties with organisation, teachers may be able to reduce some of the barriers to learning that learners with ASD may face.

In summary, the work system promotes personal, social and emotional development, including independence in carrying out activities, independence in the environment, independent use of resources, concentration and sitting quietly. Key curriculum skills include communication and working with others; both can be facilitated through the use of work systems. Work systems are excellent strategies for developing these organisation and study skills. Personal, social and health education, including managing one's own behaviour, self-control, personal autonomy, making choices, taking responsibility and feeling positive, can all be facilitated through the work system. Finally, another aspect of the school curriculum that the work system can promote is work-related learning.

Chapter 7 reviews visual structure and information and its value in accessing the curriculum. Visual structure can be used to differentiate tasks for learners with ASD helping to organise, clarify and highlight important and relevant information. It can be extremely helpful for instructing learners about how to complete specific tasks and how to use required materials. Research has repeatedly demonstrated that people with ASD learn best when materials are presented visually so these visual tasks are the best ways to promote learning and understanding.

The principles of inclusion include the need to set suitable learning challenges, overcome potential barriers to learning and respond to individual learning needs.

Structured Teaching, and especially its use of visual structure, adapts visual materials, activities and tasks to the appropriate developmental level for each individual learner.

Adaptations, clarification and organisation of materials are especially helpful for younger learners. Examples illustrate how visually structured activities can help learners develop basic skills within an Early Years curriculum, for example mathematical development or hand–eye coordination. Similar clarification and organisation are helpful to learners with ASD and additional learning difficulties.

Visual structure can also help learners to achieve in specific subject lessons. For example, visual organisation, clarity and instructions may enable learners to engage in experimentation and investigation in science, using a range of equipment in familiar and relevant situations. In mathematics and numeracy lessons, visual cues can highlight relevant information to keep learners focused and engaged and may, for example, remind learners which operations they need to use. Structured activities also help with literacy, for example writing about events and personal experiences linked to a variety of familiar incidents from stories using a prepared visual template. Visual instructions can be incorporated into PE lessons, for example in activities requiring learners to perform basic skills in travelling, and choosing and linking skills and actions in short movement phases. In design and technology, visual cues enable learners to assemble, join and combine materials or to plan, make and reflect.

Visual cues can encourage learners to solve simple problems and develop early thinking skills, and provide learners with opportunities to be involved with visual and/or tactile recording that reflect their widening range of experiences.

Visual information is also helpful outside the classroom. For example, it can promote the work of learners in developing their entrepreneurial skills, to prepare learners for broadening their experiences and in work-related learning.

Visual symbols can also be helpful in monitoring behaviours in a wide range of contexts. For example, highlighting important information can also be helpful in achieving targets in personal education relating to personal hygiene.

Clearly these visual strategies can help learners to access a very wide range of curriculum areas. The principle underpinning these approaches emphasises the importance of individualised assessment. In order to develop the most effective levels of structure for a learner, it is essential that careful assessment of the individual needs of the learner be carried out. This will include an assessment of the learner's level of visual cognition and what degree of structure ensures greatest understanding and independence. The four elements of Structured Teaching then combine to provide the learner with the level of structure that helps him to understand and to access the curriculum. Different learners will have different requirements, hence the examples in this book serve only to illustrate how the approach can be used. The challenge now is to assess individual needs and to develop structured approaches that facilitate teaching and learning for each individual.

It is also crucial to regularly monitor and assess the levels of structure a learner is using. A learner's needs will change over time and different levels of structure may be required for some learners in different contexts. For example, a learner may need greater structure in an unfamiliar classroom with unfamiliar peers, or when he enters a new context such as work experience. While some learners may need constant levels of structure for a long period, others may have fairly rapidly changing requirements. This can only be provided through careful monitoring of the structure.

Finally, independent tasks also need to be monitored carefully. While some learners will benefit from some repetition, others may become bored if they are required to repeat tasks too often. Progress needs to be assessed and monitored to record learner progression. In addition, independent tasks should be linked to areas of learning and referenced to specific aspects of the curriculum. For example, a learner may have a series of tasks for independent work during literacy lessons. Tasks may relate to the literacy lesson and should be cross-referenced to the literacy curriculum or linked to a learner's individual targets. Either way, the learner's progress needs to be monitored and recorded.

The short summary and review in this chapter only touches the surface. There are undoubtedly numerous other ways that the Structured Teaching approach can support, enhance and facilitate implementation of the curriculum. A real strength of Structured Teaching is its ability to combine with a number of other approaches, philosophies or curricula to enhance the development of learners with ASD. Structured Teaching provides a framework for delivering the curriculum for learners with specific learning styles. Within this framework, the content of the curriculum can be, and should be, broad and balanced. If the *framework* of Structured Teaching is used to deliver the curriculum, opportunities can then be provided for learners with ASD to access a curriculum that is appropriate for their needs, including varied approaches such as music interaction therapy, physical exercise and social skills programmes.

Structured Teaching is an 'autism friendly' way of organising and presenting information to people with ASD. Deriving its strategies from the growing literature on the neurological basis of autism, Structured Teaching offers countless strategies, approaches and techniques that those involved in teaching or supporting learners with ASD will find extremely helpful. The examples offered in this book are just a starting point of what can be accomplished. Hopefully, these examples will inspire teachers, parents and other interested professionals, who are starting with the exciting task of providing learners with ASD access to the many rich and important opportunities that the whole curriculum should provide.

Chapter 9

Increasing curriculum access by blending Structured Teaching with other strategies

Introduction

Structured Teaching was created by Eric Schopler and Division TEACCH as an alternative to the psychodynamic approach that was the dominant intervention strategy for those with autism spectrum disorders (ASD) in the 1960s. Schopler's idea was that people with ASD think, learn and understand differently from 'typical' people so that interventions had to modify learning environments, materials and organisational strategies to make them more autism-friendly. He thought that these children could function in educational settings and in later life in their communities if exposed to educational approaches that were sensitive to their learning styles. This idea was initially embraced by many who were very uncomfortable with the psychodynamic approaches of the day.

Because Structured Teaching was one of the first alternative approaches to the psychodynamic intervention models, Schopler and his colleagues went on to create ways in which this idea could be useful for parents in the home and for schools in the community. These ideas of creating autism-friendly materials and environments were organised into a series of systematic strategies called Structured Teaching. Structured Teaching strategies have been widely applied and continue to be among the most commonly used evidence-based approaches to helping people with ASD at home and in the community. This has made Structured Teaching a very effective and widely applied intervention strategy all over the world.

Another reason why Structured Teaching has had wide acceptance is that the basic idea behind Structured Teaching is to make the world more autism-friendly for people with ASD by making adaptations that accommodate their learning. This idea also has wide applications beyond the Structured Teaching model. In fact, as this chapter will demonstrate, Structured Teaching ideas can be blended with many other systems by educators because the elements of Structured Teaching are all based on making the world make more sense to people with ASD and helping them to think, learn and understand more effectively. Therefore any approach can be supplemented by the ideas in Structured Teaching that help make the world more autism-friendly for people with ASD.

Blending Structured Teaching with other approaches and strategies

There are a wide range of approaches and strategies that are easily blended with Structured Teaching and in particular those strategies which use visual cues. For example, Ricky (age six) is quickly developing visual skills which might be used to support his communication through visual communication strategies such as the Picture Exchange Communication System (PECS) (Bondy and Frost 1994). However some other approaches may, at first glance, seem contradictory to the structure of Structured Teaching. This chapter includes examples of blending Structured Teaching with other visual strategies and also with approaches which may seem less straightforward to blend. This includes strategies to: enhance child-led interaction; develop social communication and emotional regulation; develop social understanding; develop cooperative group work and address anxieties which create barriers to curriculum access.

Case study

Structured Teaching and interaction approaches

Sam is three years old and has a diagnosis of autism and learning difficulties. He attends an integrated nursery where he is supported full time by a learning support assistant. Sam's structure is summarised in Table 9.1.

Table 9.1 Summary of structure for Sam

Physical structure	Areas of classroom designated for specific purposes; use of furniture and screens define specific areas for specific activities and reduce distractions. Distraction-free work bay; labelled chair with photo. Carpet square to show where to sit during group and class activities.
Schedule	Transition objects which are handed to him prior to an activity; beginning of 'first, then' routine.
Work system	Left to right work system with finished box.
Visual information	Visually structured tasks ('shoebox tasks').

Structured Teaching is used to create an effective learning environment for Sam and aims to help him feel safe and secure. This structure provides positive routines, reduces distractions and helps him to concentrate in what would otherwise feel like a very chaotic environment for him. Structure provides organisation and support which enable him to begin to be independent and to succeed in completing early learning tasks. Sam is taught how to use structured strategies which will help him to be ready to learn.

Whilst learning how to use the structure is a priority for Sam, another priority is for him to develop positive relationships with staff, and in the first instance with a key worker. When Sam first joined the nursery setting, he was fearful of adults and children; establishing a positive relationship with an adult is a crucial step towards enabling Sam to be ready to learn and to access the breadth of the Early Years curriculum which includes interacting positively and appropriately with children and adults.

Structured Teaching and interaction approaches: following Sam's lead

Interaction approaches which begin with following the child's lead offer a useful 'way in' to engage a child such as Sam who is isolated from and fearful of other people. Child-led interaction approaches aim to build positive, mutually enjoyable interaction routines, through strategies which replicate early social interactions between infants and carers. A variety of approaches advocate child-led interactions, for example Intensive Interaction (Hewett *et al.* 2011), Floortime (Greenspan and Wieder 2006) and the Early Start Denver Model (ESDM) (Rogers and Dawson 2010). Such approaches suggest that adults should join the child in his or her activities in order for the child to become more aware of others and to experience enjoyable social interactions. The ESDM for example advocates teaching joint activity play routines by mimicking caregiver–infant interactions such as: attention to parent faces and voices; parent–child interactions that attract infants' attention, bringing smiles and delight to both; parent imitation of infant sounds and intentional actions; parent use of toys to support, rather than compete with, the child's social attention.

Child-led approaches require adults to be responsive to a child's movements, actions and interests and are more spontaneous than the more organised strategies of Structured Teaching. Indeed, it might be assumed that interaction approaches are the antithesis to Structured Teaching and as such these two are not easily combined with one another. However, this need not be the case and it may be possible, and to a child's benefit, to combine these so-called 'opposing' approaches. In Sam's case, whilst he is learning to use structured approaches which help him to feel safe and to begin to develop some independence, at the same time he also needs to build positive relationships which lay the foundations for being able to 'work with others' across the breadth of the curriculum. The following example illustrates how Structured Teaching and interaction approaches are combined to provide Sam with both structured learning and spontaneous interaction routines.

A support assistant, Jo, is allocated as a key worker for Sam. She sets up the physical structure for Sam each day, making sure his work bay is free from clutter and that tasks are ready on a shelf. Jo has been observing Sam closely to decide which objects have meaning for him for each activity; from her observations she has identified a number of objects she can give to Sam to support transitions between activities (see Chapter 5). Sam accepts the objects and is able to independently locate the sand tray, outside play and his work bay. He completes one activity independently, especially when the activity incorporates his favourite TV character; Jo gestures to the finished box to prompt 'finished', then gives Sam an object to transition to his next activity. Sam has quickly learned this work routine and has been observed smiling when reaching for his task; he has also been heard humming a tune from a TV programme which his mum says he loves to watch at home. Sam has become familiar and comfortable with the nursery layout and Jo feels he is less anxious as he is able to predict and understand routine activities.

Now that Sam seems to be more at ease, the nursery teacher suggests that Jo could now begin to develop social interaction play with Sam. Jo has attended inset training on interaction approaches and decides to follow Sam's lead and try to join in his activities by copying his actions and sounds. Jo observes Sam and identifies some actions and activities which he seems to enjoy, including: flapping his hands and humming a TV tune, wafting silky scarves, pushing soft toys down a slide. Jo approaches Sam in the play area and copies his actions and activities. The first time Sam appears to notice Jo is when she flaps her hands and hums the same TV tune; he pauses and makes fleeting eye contact then continues with his flapping and humming. Jo copies Sam in his activities several times each day, gradually building up to using a pause-burst routine 'ready, steady...', waiting for Sam to indicate 'go'. Sam enjoys these activities and especially likes Jo to waft silky scarves over his head. Jo continues to join Sam in his activities on a regular basis, usually when he is in the play area. Sam sometimes approaches Jo and offers her a scarf or a soft toy which Jo interprets as 'play with me'.

To incorporate these social play sessions into Sam's day, Jo decides to use a silky scarf as a transition object. When Sam has finished his work, she gives him a scarf to transition to play where she then joins him in his activities. In addition, a scarf is attached to a screen next to the play area and the teacher is teaching Sam to request 'play with me' by taking the scarf to Jo.

Sam's day is structured to help him to feel safe and to be able to develop some independence; Structured Teaching approaches provide a learning environment which is meaningful to Sam and which is helping him to develop key skills. Within this structure, interaction approaches are incorporated into Sam's day which foster mutually enjoyable interactions with his key worker; fostering positive relationships is an essential precursor to being able to work with others across the curriculum. Whilst presently Jo initiates most of the play sessions, it is intended that Sam will be able to request 'play with me' when in the play area. The distinction between work and play needs to be clear for Sam and in the future he will be taught to follow 'first work, then play' in developing his ability to follow a visual schedule. The combination of structure and spontaneity enriches Sam's early education and together enable him to begin to access a broader range of activities across the curriculum.

Case study

Structured Teaching and SCERTS

Martin is 14; he has autism and attends a special school for leaners with severe learning difficulties. He is placed in a specialist class for six learners who are on the autism spectrum; whilst he spends much of his time in the class, Martin also integrates into other classes for some lessons including drama and food technology. Table 9.2 summarises Structured Teaching strategies in place for Martin.

Table 9.2 Summary of structure for Martin

Physical structure	Designated areas for specific activities; screens to reduce distractions; sits on periphery of group activities; quiet room for Martin to retreat to when overloaded.
Schedule	Part day object schedule enables Martin to follow the day's activities and has resulted in him gaining access to a broader curriculum by 'sandwiching' non-preferred activities with preferred.
Work system	Left to right work system with finished file/box; completes four tasks followed by choice of two preferred activities.
Visual information	Visually structured tasks, visual clarification strategies.

Structured Teaching strategies enable Martin to understand the sequence of activities each day and to develop independence in transitioning between activities. Whilst he sometimes becomes overwhelmed, particularly due to sensory hypersensitivities, he is learning to manage his anxiety at these times by using a 'quiet room' adjacent to the main classroom. Visual communication strategies are available to Martin at all times to encourage him to communicate his likes and dislikes, to make requests and to let staff know when he is feeling anxious.

The SCERTS approach (Prizant *et al.* 2005a, 2005b) has been adopted by the school as a broad approach which aims to develop social and communication skills and emotional regulation. In order to achieve this, the approach includes transactional supports which include support for learning and support for families and professionals. The focus of this approach on individual wellbeing is considered by the school to be highly relevant to those learners in school who have autism and severe learning difficulties, including Martin. Structured Teaching strategies are used as 'transactional supports' in that visual structure is an effective way of supporting learning. The following example illustrates how the two approaches are blended for Martin to enable him to learn and to enhance his wellbeing.

Martin's main class teacher has completed both TEACCH and SCERTS training and has developed a blended approach to meeting Martin's individual needs. The use of Structured Teaching to develop independence and self-esteem integrates well with the priorities of the SCERTS approach and are considered by Martin's teacher as an effective combination which prioritises his wellbeing. A number of strategies are blended to address this priority.

Independence and self-esteem

Developing Martin's independence is a key priority and the use of Structured Teaching strategies enables Martin to develop a number of independent skills. His independent use of an object schedule provides him with meaningful information which enables him to predict and understand his daily activities. Martin uses the same type of schedule at home at weekends and when he attends a short breaks facility, thus transferring his independence to a different context. As his independence increases, so too does his self-esteem and his parents report that he is happier and more relaxed.

Social communication

Martin makes requests and choices by giving objects to adults. Photographs are now attached to the objects which he is most familiar with, including object/photo for asking for favourite activities (iPod, tablet, aeroplane magazines, shopping catalogues). Opportunities for communicating are built into his structure, for example by offering choices of two activities when work is finished; Martin makes his choice and takes the selected object/photo to an adult to request the item he has chosen.

As Martin experiences high levels of anxiety at times, strategies to communicate his anxieties are considered to be a communication priority. In addition to having the opportunity to request access to preferred activities, he is being taught to use a visual communication key-chain to let staff know that he needs to use the quiet room. The key-chain is attached to his trouser waist-band so that he has access to it at all times. A mini-object and photograph of a rocking chair which Martin likes to use in the quiet room is attached to a duplicate photograph on the key-chain; Martin is observed closely and at the first signs of anxiety (increased flapping and rocking) he is prompted to pull off the object/photo and give it to an adult. He is then able to go to the quiet room where he can rock on the rocking chair and/or look at a shopping catalogue. Whilst this strategy is currently prompted, the aim is for Martin to be able to request access to the quiet room whenever he needs to; once he has learned to do this independently, staff will liaise with home and staff at the short break facility to provide opportunities to transfer this important communication skill.

Emotional regulation

In addition to teaching Martin how to communicate that he needs the quiet room, it is important for him to learn strategies that will enable him to regulate or manage his emotional state, particularly when he is anxious. As Martin likes to play with a variety of sensory 'toys', such as a squeezy stress ball, a sensory box is provided from which he can select items which he can 'fiddle' with. This box is offered at regular intervals as part of Martin's choices; in addition, he is offered items from the sensory box at those times he finds difficult, for example at times when he has to wait or during whole-class lessons. The sensory toys appear to ease Martin's anxieties and aid his concentration during whole-class parts of a lesson. Martin has access to the same types of sensory toys at home and at the short break facility to ensure a consistent approach.

The above strategies are just a few of the combination which are implemented to enable Martin to learn, to communicate and to express and manage his anxieties and emotions. The blending of strategies complements the aims and principles of both TEACCH Structured Teaching and SCERTS approaches and together enhance provision and practice with Martin's wellbeing at the centre. Enhancing Martin's independence and self-esteem is related to overcoming barriers to curriculum access, whilst providing him with meaningful social communication and emotional regulation strategies mean he is less anxious and has greater autonomy. Prioritising Martin's wellbeing in this way means he is supported in order to be *ready to learn* across all aspects of the curriculum.

Case study

Structured Teaching, social scripts and Social Stories

Sofie is ten years old and attends a local mainstream school in a town in Denmark. She is currently in a class of 21 learners and she has five hours of additional support during the week. Sofie is achieving expected levels in all subjects. Whilst she is academically able, she experiences difficulties with organisation and sequencing skills and has particular difficulties with knowing where to focus her attention during taught lessons. Structured Teaching strategies enable Sofie to access a broad curriculum, including the social aspects of school life. Table 9.3 summarises Structured Teaching strategies in place for Sofie.

Table 9.3 Summary of structure for Sofie

Physical structure	Classroom layout and seating position clearly identified to reduce anxieties and distractions, with easy exit accessible. Safe space and use of adjacent room to observe whole-school activities.
Schedule	Written schedule using electronic calendar. Weekly and daily schedule information available by using a tablet. Activity folders for Sofie to access during unstructured time.
Work system	Written work system in notebook. Plans to integrate this with electronic schedule information using a tablet.
Visual information	Written instructions across curriculum; visual clarification strategies to focus attention to detail, e.g. on worksheets.

Structured Teaching strategies enable Sofie to access the curriculum by creating an effective learning environment and by providing information in ways which are meaningful and motivating for Sofie. As a result, she is able to access all subject lessons; at the same time the structure supports key skills and for Sofie this includes support for the development of social skills. Working with others is a particular challenge for Sofie and the difficulties she has with working with her peers creates barriers to curriculum access.

In order to support Sofie with learning key social skills, which are essential for her to participate in paired, group and class work across the curriculum, the autism consultant and class teacher discussed how best to support these important skills. As working with others is difficult for Sofie, the adults agreed that any strategy they introduced would need to be motivating. They decided to teach Sofie to use a social script, with a visual cue as a reminder, and then to consider how they might include social scripts and reminders on her tablet. The following example illustrates the blending of Structured Teaching with social scripts and the use of technology to motivate Sofie. The example shows the first stage in teaching Sofie to use the social skill of taking turns and then demonstrates how this can be extended to help Sofie to develop her social understanding by writing a Social Story (Gray 2010).

Sofie is allowed to play games on a computer with a classmate during one break time each day. The physical structure ensures the learning environment is comfortable for Sofie and her schedule identifies when this activity takes place. Sofie loves using the computer and so is highly motivated by the activity; in particular she likes games which include animated characters. As a way to increase her social engagement with her peers, a classmate is invited each day to play games with Sofie on the computer during break time. Sofie's peers are keen to join her in this activity and so there are always plenty who volunteer to join in.

Social script – reminders for what to do

As Sofie is highly motivated by using the computer, and this makes good use of her strengths and interests, the teacher and consultant felt that this activity offers an opportunity for Sofie to work with a peer. During class lessons Sofie finds working with her peers difficult and usually refuses to do so. The first step to teach Sofie the skills required to work with peers was to work alongside a peer during an activity which she enjoyed. However, it quickly became clear that Sofie is unable to take turns; in particular, as the games progress through levels of difficulty, Sofie insists on interrupting her peer's turn in order to complete every level as quickly as possible. Likewise, if her classmate is having a turn and something goes wrong, Sofie takes over in a bid to complete the game successfully. It is clear that in this context, whilst the structure supports participation in this activity to some extent, other strategies are also required to teach Sofie the skills which she currently lacks or forgets.

A short written script was introduced to Sofie to remind her of the structure of the activity and that she has to take turns with her classmate (see Figure 9.1). Just before break, Sofie is prompted to read the script; the visual cue 'remember' card (see Figure 9.2) is placed on the computer desk. This strategy blends well with Structured Teaching as both use the visual strengths of the individual.

Social Story – understanding why

The social script and visual cue are helpful in reminding Sofie what she has to do, however the social script does not help her to understand why she needs to take turns. For this reason, the next step is to write a personalised Social Story (see Figure 9.3) which explains how people feel if children do not take turns. Social Stories or Articles blend well with Structured Teaching strategies due to the visual component. Moreover, the structure can provide reminders which directly link to the Social Story; for example the schedule could include a reminder: 'remember to take turns in lessons and games'. Alternatively the schedule might include a message: 'Taking turns is important'. Each time Sofie checks her schedule, she will see the reminder which helps her to recall the Social Story content.

A further example illustrates the value of combining Structured Teaching and Social Stories. A visual, written cue reminds Sarah of the skills needed to work with others (see Chapter 7 and Figure 9.4).

A Social Article (see Figure 9.5) enhances this by providing written information which explains **why** these skills are important to remember.

Turn-taking

In my ___ o'clock break I am allowed to play games on the computer.

I am allowed to choose a friend to play the game with me.

I play with either _____ or _____.

First we choose the game we want to play, **then** we play.

We **take turns** playing the levels in the game.

Take turns means that when I finish a level, it is my friend's turn to play the next level.

When it is my **friend's turn**, I need to give the keyboard to my friend.

When my friend finishes a level, it is my turn. My friend will give me the keyboard.

Taking turns goes on until the game is completed or if break time ends.

Try to remember to let my friend have a turn and complete her level.

Figure 9.1 Social script for turn-taking at break time.

Remember

Take turns

When I have finished a level, give the keyboard to my friend.

Let my friend finish her level.

Figure 9.2 Visual cue as a reminder to take turns.

The blending of Structured Teaching, social scripts and Social Stories enables individuals to develop key skills, in Sofie's and Sarah's cases the approaches enables them to develop important social skills and to understand why these skills are important. Lack of key skills creates barriers to curriculum access; strategies which help individuals to learn these skills have the potential to support learners like Sofie and Sarah to participate in all aspects of the curriculum.

Why children need to take turns in lessons and at break times.

Children at _____ school often need to take turns.

They take turns when they play games at break time.

They take turns when they work in a group and when the teacher teaches the whole class.

These are examples of lessons when children have to take turns: literacy, mathematics, art, science.

Children would all like a turn – they would like a turn to play, to speak, to ask a question, to answer a question, to tell the teacher what they know.

<u>Taking turns is important.</u>

For example:
If everyone speaks at the same time, the teacher would not be able to hear what children are saying.

If children do not let others have their turn, their friends may be upset. They might think:

I did not have my turn.

It's not fair.

Our teacher would like all children to take turns when they play games and in lessons.

<u>I will try to remember to take turns in lessons and at break times.</u>
When I need to take turns, the teacher will usually remind me. I can look at my social script and my 'remember' card if I forget what to do.

When children take turns, everyone has a chance to play, to speak or to ask or answer questions. This helps everyone to feel that break time and lessons are fair. Our teacher is very pleased when children remember to take turns. Taking turns often helps children and teachers to feel happy.

Figure 9.3 Social Story to teach why children need to take turns.

1.   Listen to what others have to say.

2.   Take turns in the conversation.

3.   Speak in a volume that is comfortable for others.

4.   Ask questions when it is your turn.

5.   Try to say positive and kind words about other children's ideas.

Figure 9.4 Visual cue: reminder of skills needed to work with other children.

Working with other children.

Learning to work with other children is important. The teacher often plans for children to work together in lessons. Children sometimes work in pairs or in groups of four, five or six.

Sometimes children forget what they need to do to work with other children. When children forget, they may read a reminder. Here is my reminder for what I need to do and why it is important:

1.   Listen to what others have to say *BECAUSE then you will know what other children think.*

2.   Take turns in the conversation *BECAUSE then everyone will have a chance of a turn.*

3.   Speak in a volume that is comfortable for others *BECAUSE they will feel safe and relaxed while listening.*

4.   Ask questions when it is your turn *BECAUSE then everyone will have a chance to ask a question.*

5.   Try to say positive and kind words about other children's ideas *BECAUSE children often feel friendly about people who use kind words.* Examples could be: **"good try"**, **"I like your idea"**.

Figure 9.5 Social Article to teach why skills are needed to work with other children.

Most children like to have a turn to speak and to ask questions. Children who do not have a turn may feel upset and they may feel it is unfair. Many children like to have a turn. When children have a turn the teacher finds out what different children think and know.

I will try to <u>remember</u>, it is my turn when someone looks at me and pauses, or if they ask me a question. If I forget, someone will give me a 'your turn' card. If it is not my turn and I have something important to say, I can write it in my 'ideas and questions' notebook. I can show the teacher my notebook later in the lesson. Children and adults in our class will feel that it is fairer when all children have a chance for their turns.

Figure 9.5 Continued

Planning for effective group work and developing cooperative work is important across curriculum subjects. This is often one of the more challenging aspects of teaching and learning to plan and implement due to the difficulties which group work pose for learners on the spectrum. The following examples illustrate how 'jisgaw' planning can be strengthened by also including Structured Teaching strategies. The examples given include a vocational group activity and a food technology group activity; however, the principles which underpin this particular combination of strategies can be applied to group work across the curriculum.

Case study

Structured Teaching and jigsaw planning

Kulpreet, Deepak, Ahmed and Sanjay are young adults aged 18–19 who attend a specialist educational setting for learners on the autism spectrum in India. They attend the educational setting daily and they participate in a variety of activities including vocational training. The vocational aspect of the curriculum is a priority, with the aim of preparing young adults to participate in work-related activities in the local community. Table 9.4 summarises Structured Teaching strategies in place to enable cooperative group work.

Structured Teaching strategies have enabled these students to work cooperatively and to utilise their vocational skills in order to complete a group task. However, Structured Teaching was not used in isolation as the teacher considered how to plan this cooperative activity. Participation in group work, across the curriculum, presents particular challenges to learners on the autism spectrum due to their difficulties with communication and interaction. However, group work also provides opportunities for individuals to learn a number of skills which are essential throughout life. Being able to cooperate and work with other is essential if individuals are to participate in both educational and community activities.

Successful group work creates interdependence between participants and is planned to ensure all members of a group are able to fulfil their role in a group task. One

Table 9.4 Summary of structure for Kulpreet, Deepak, Ahmed and Sanjay

Physical structure	Adjacent tables placed in row for three of the four students. A low level screen reduces some distractions but does not entirely obscure the view of the open teaching space.
Schedule	Symbol/word daily schedules. Group work symbol also includes names and photos of the students who are working together for the cooperative task.
	One student uses a shorter schedule. For this task, Sanjay's schedule shows the less preferred activity (job) sandwiched between preferred activities (lunch and choose).
Work system	Left to right group work system; each student completes his task and places item in a basket to their right which becomes next student's work materials. A final finished basket at the end of the row becomes Sanjay's job after lunch. Sanjay is not yet able to sit adjacently to the other students so the basket of post is brought to him at his teaching table. The aim is to eventually adjust the structure until Sanjay feels comfortable sitting at the end of the work row.
Visual information	Combination of symbols and words provides sequence of steps for whole task (which is attached to the low level screen) and instructions for each student to complete his part of the task.

approach which is helpful in considering how to plan for the challenge of group work is jigsaw planning. This planning approach identifies particular roles and tasks for individuals or groups, with the aim to promote interdependence among group members. By creating interdependence, this encourages group members to support and encourage each other in order for the group to succeed. Howley and Rose (2003) suggest that:

> the jigsaw approach enables the teacher to plan to meet individual needs within a purposeful group activity, centred upon the strengths and interests of the pupil. In addition, structured teaching approaches may further empower the pupil to participate in what is potentially a stressful learning environment.
>
> (p. 22)

Jigsaw planning and Structured Teaching work well together in order to plan for successful group participation, as indicated in the following steps:

- Allocate the learner with autism a task which is an essential component of the group activity and which best utilises the individual's strengths and/or interests. This task should be one which the learner is capable of achieving as the learning objectives should link to key skills for group work.
- Identify learning objectives for the individual which are linked to social and/or communication skills and which are essential key skills to be able to participate successfully as a group member.
- Consider each component of Structured Teaching which can be implemented to support the individual in achieving the goal of working as part of a group.

The example which follows demonstrates how jigsaw planning and Structured Teaching strategies were combined to support Kulpreet, Deepak, Ahmed and Sanjay to participate in cooperative group work.

In order for Kulpreet, Deepak, Ahmed and Sanjay to participate in group work, the teacher planned the mailing activity as follows:

- Individual tasks are identified as essential components of the mailing job; these were identified through task analysis.
- Each task is allocated to individuals according to their independent skills. Each task forms one piece of the 'mailing job jigsaw'; as each task is an essential part of the mailing job, the students are reliant upon each other to complete the whole job.
- Structured Teaching components are planned according to individual needs and strengths (see Table 9.4).
- Further visual information is provided to show the students the complete 'mailing job jigsaw' which is attached to the low-level screen (see Figure 9.6).

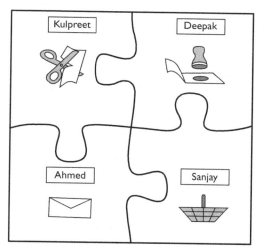

Figure 9.6 Jigsaw plan for cooperative group work.

- When the three students transition to the group work area, one piece of the 'mailing job jigsaw' is available on the student's desk. This puzzle piece visually reminds the individual of his job.
- When the individual completes his task, he fixes his jigsaw piece to the 'mailing job jigsaw'. This helps each individual to see how his work contributes to the whole job.
- After lunch, Sanjay is given a puzzle piece which visually represents his job of delivering the post (i.e. the basket of mail). On his return, he is prompted by the TA to fix his puzzle piece to the 'mailing job jigsaw', thus adding the final piece.
- When the mailing job is complete, the four students are gathered and the teacher shows them the completed puzzle. This is used to encourage each student to recall his part of the task and to praise the group for completing their mailing job. The visual representation of the overall job as a jigsaw puzzle proved motivating to these students as they liked to see the puzzle completed.

Whilst this example illustrates how jigsaw planning and Structured Teaching are combined to plan and support a vocational group activity, the same principles and strategies can be applied to planning and supporting group work across curriculum subjects. For example, Sarah's teacher used jigsaw planning to enable Sarah to fully participate in a class activity to create a sports day newsletter (see Chapter 7). This meant that Sarah was given a role that was essential for her group to complete their task. Sarah was allocated a task which used her strengths and interests and which encouraged communication between her and her peers. Written instructions and visual reminders provided meaningful information which supported her participation in what is potentially stressful group work (see Figures 7.35 and 7.36).

The following example illustrates how jigsaw planning and Structured Teaching support Leila to participate in group work during two food technology lessons.

Case study

Leila is nine years old and has autism and learning difficulties. She attends specialist provision within a mainstream school and integrates into some mainstream class lessons. Structured Teaching strategies for Leila include: an independent work table, adjacent to another, in the mainstream class; part-day symbol schedule; number-matching work system; visual information which clarifies important information within a task and symbol/word instructions.

As Leila's integration into the mainstream class has become increasingly successful, it is decided that she could be supported to participate in small group work. The teacher is planning a series of two lessons in food technology in which the children are to research healthy foods and to plan, and make items for, a healthy picnic basket. The class is organised into groups of four and each group are to present their picnic basket to the class.

By jigsaw planning the lesson, the teacher allocates roles to individuals in each group. Leila is given tasks which make use of her skills and preferences (Mum reports that she loves making her sandwiches for school each morning). These tasks are essential to her group's success, thus creating interdependency and so her peers are likely to encourage her. Figure 9.7 illustrates the jigsaw plan for Leila's group. This jigsaw is placed for the group to see and acts as a visual reminder of each person's role in achieving the whole group task of researching and making a healthy picnic.

Leila's targets for this activity are identified as: (1) to share working space with two peers; (2) to communicate with a partner (Jake) when items are sliced; (3) to take part in a presentation to the class by showing her group's products.

Structured Teaching strategies promote Leila's independence and provide information and instructions which are meaningful to her. These strategies include:

- Physical structure:
  - Lesson 1 single use of computer, positioned adjacent to Jake who uses a separate computer.
  - Lesson 2 place at corner of group table with space either side of Leila; during presentation seated at the periphery of the class, near to the reading corner where she can retreat if too anxious.
  - Schedule: symbol/words; photos and names of group members; activity following lesson is to use the quiet reading corner which Leila likes.
- Work system:
  - Lesson 1: numbered symbols to show 'look', 'choose 2 fillings'. Timer set to show how long to look for healthy fillings. Symbol for Leila to tell TA when finished.

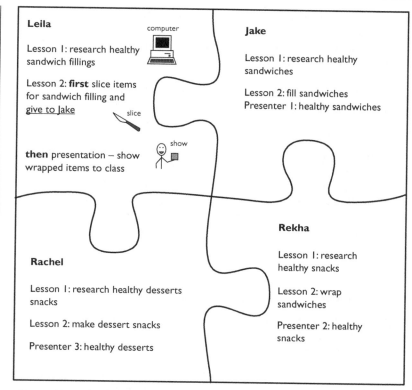

Researching and making a healthy picnic.

Figure 9.7 Jigsaw for group food technology activity – Leila's group.

- Lesson 2: left to right organisation – food items and tools in basket on left, finished plate on right; this is a simpler system than Leila's usual system as group work is more stressful for her.
- Presentation: wrapped food items are numbered in a picnic basket for Leila to show to the class and return to basket.
- Visual information:
  - Lesson 1: symbol/word instructions.
  - Lesson 2: visual clarification and organisation for task, highlighted visual rules for safe use of knife when slicing.
  - Presentation: visual cues (numbered) for showing items to class during her group's presentation. Visual reminder to go to reading corner if anxious.

These examples illustrate an approach to planning group work which often presents particular barriers to curriculum access for learners on the autism spectrum; at the same time, participation in group work is an important part of the curriculum for learners on the spectrum. In summary:

- Jigsaw planning allocates roles to create interdependency between group members.

- Interdependency promotes peer-to-peer encouragement.
- Tasks are allocated according to an individual's strengths and interests.
- Structured Teaching provides the individual with familiar strategies of which provide support for participating in group work.

Note that as group work often raises anxiety levels for individuals on the spectrum, Structured Teaching strategies may need adjusting to acknowledge this anxiety. For example, a learner who is usually able to read written instructions may need additional symbols when participating in group work.

Managing anxieties is essential to improving curriculum access. If learners are anxious and worried, this creates barriers to curriculum access – nobody learns if they feel anxious and so Structured Teaching strategies are important for reducing anxiety by increasing independence and self-esteem. The following examples illustrate how other strategies blend with Structured Teaching in order to reduce anxiety, build confidence and independence, and promote self-esteem and wellbeing.

Case study

Structured Teaching and strategies for managing worries and anxieties

Emily is 15 years old and attends a non-profit private elementary and secondary learning centre in North Carolina which is geared to children who need structure, consistency, positive reinforcement, more movement, reduced stress, both remediation and challenge along with a multi-sensory way of learning. Whilst Emily is not distracted by her environment, she is often preoccupied with and distracted by 'worries' and anxieties which result in her feeling upset. Emily responds well to Structured Teaching strategies and her schedule and work system are used to help her to focus upon 'what' and 'how much'. Table 9.5 summarises Emily's structure.

Table 9.5 Summary of structure for Emily

Physical structure	Individual work station.
Schedule	Written schedule with directions to work system for each lesson.
Work system	Portable written work system on clipboard.
Visual information	Picture/written instructions.
	Use of a tablet using a presentation programme.

The previous chapters illustrate how Emily's structure helps her to focus and to be independent and also encourage participation on curriculum activities which she may otherwise resist. While these strategies do alleviate Emily's anxieties, a variety of other strategies are implemented in combination with Structured Teaching.

Emily uses her structure independently and with confidence on 'good' days; however, she still worries and becomes anxious and whilst refocusing her back to her structure reassures her, further strategies are introduced to support Emily's wellbeing.

Visual cues and relaxation strategies

Emily has been taught to complete a relaxation exercise at times when she is worried, anxious or upset. This includes squeezing a stress ball, breathing exercises, yoga and spending time on one of her favourite activities (colouring pictures). This combination of strategies is supported with a variety of visual cues and a visual narrative to remind Emily to use her strategies to stay calm and relaxed. Figure 9.8 illustrates the exercise routine, presented with visual instructions and cues, which Emily follows independently. This example illustrates how the combination of strategies may be more effective than each strategy used in isolation.

Staying calm and relaxed helps keep my body healthy
and happy. I can do relaxation exercises to keep me
calm.

First, I can squeeze my squishy balls 5 times 1 – 2 – 3 – 4 – 5

Next I can take 5 very slow deep breaths

Then I can squeeze my squishy balls 5 more times 1 – 2 – 3 – 4 – 5

I can take 5 more very slow deep breaths

Colouring helps me stay calm.

I did a GREAT job of practicing my relaxation!

I am proud of myself and ready to work!

Figure 9.8 Relaxation exercise.

Similarly, as Emily has learned a range of yoga poses, these are visually represented to remind her of how to use this strategy on a regular basis to help her to feel calm (see Figure 9.9).

Access to a broad curriculum is dependent upon an individual's wellbeing. Structured Teaching strategies, combined with techniques to teach learners to self-calm, are essential to encourage individuals to participate in a variety of curriculum lessons. The following example (Adam) also illustrates blending of Structured Teaching with other strategies to reduce anxieties which create barriers to curriculum access.

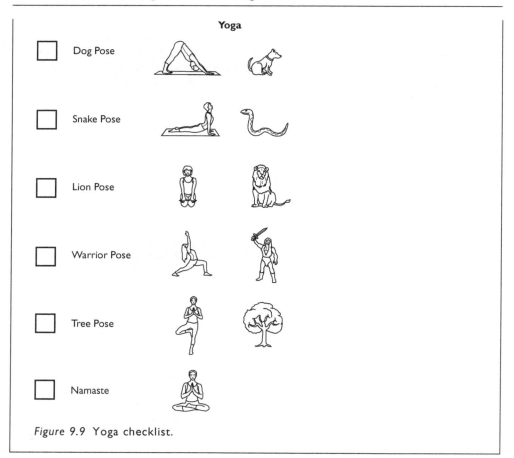

Yoga

- ☐ Dog Pose
- ☐ Snake Pose
- ☐ Lion Pose
- ☐ Warrior Pose
- ☐ Tree Pose
- ☐ Namaste

Figure 9.9 Yoga checklist.

Case study

Adam is 15 years old and has Asperger Syndrome. He attends a local mainstream secondary school where he is fully included in curriculum subject lessons. Structured Teaching strategies in place for Adam are summarised in Table 9.6.

Adam has additional support at the school's learning support base; staff in this support base pre-teach Adam to prepare him for new concepts and vocabulary which facilitates his inclusion in mainstream lessons. They also prepare visual supports for a variety of lessons and also to teach him self-management strategies when he is anxious. For example, written instructions which were emailed to Adam to help him to prepare for a sixth-form presentation evening and remind him of strategies to use if anxious (see Figure 7.41).

Many students like Adam experience frequent anxieties which may be supported with Structured Teaching strategies by providing meaningful information about what to expect in a wide range of learning contexts. Adam has become increasingly skilled in using the school's VLE and accesses this via a tablet. Staff are encouraging this so that if he gains a place at university, using a tablet will not look out of place, indeed it may help facilitate his inclusion. Adam is expected to do well academically and teachers believe he will be successful in gaining a university place. However, although his anxieties are somewhat

Table 9.6 Summary of structure for Adam

Physical structure	Seating plans, clear exit routes, campus map with routes between buildings highlighted.
Schedule	Written schedule combined with work system. Schedule has been included in student planner and is now available on school's VLE.
Work system	Work system is combined with schedule and available in planner and on VLE.
Visual information	Written instructions and reminders. Visual clarification strategies such as highlighting and use of diagrams.

alleviated when he is prepared and understands expectations, Adam still experiences high levels of anxiety regularly. Staff are concerned that his anxieties may create barriers to future success, especially as when he is very anxious his mannerisms increase, including excessive throat-clearing and on occasion banging his forehead with the palm of his hand. The following example illustrates how high levels of anxiety can be supported by combining Structured Teaching with other anxiety reducing strategies.

Whilst Adam is succeeding in his academic studies, barriers to curriculum access are created by his frequent anxieties and his difficulties in communicating these anxieties when they arise. In particular, he becomes anxious about completing homework, partly because he is easily overloaded by information and details when researching for an assignment. In addition, he is often anxious when the social and communication demands in lessons are high, for example during a whole-class debate. Finally, his anxieties often increase during less structured and social times of the day such as breaks.

Written instructions and reminders are helpful in preparing Adam for events and expectations, but these are not always predictable. Future challenges will arise as more demands are made of Adam as an adult. Staff in the support base try out strategies with Adam to identify which he feels comfortable with and is able to use as and when he becomes anxious. This resulted in what Adam calls a 'menu of anxiety-busting tips for feeling confident' and included the following:

1   **Homework:** Adam is taught to use a visual mind-mapping app to help him to structure his ideas when researching topics. Structured Teaching strategies work in conjunction with the mind-mapping tool by setting boundaries and time limits for researching the topic (see Figure 9.10). A TA in the support base spends time with Adam's mum to teach her how to use the mind-mapping app and the homework template so that this strategy is transferred to homework.

2   **Social and communication demands in lessons:** Adam tries out a variety of sensory feedback tools to see if any help him to feel calmer. He selects a 'tangle-toy' (Adam calls it a 'tangler') which he is allowed to twist between his fingers during what are for him stressful points in a lesson. This strategy helps him to remain calm which then supports him to use visual supports that remind him of social and conversation rules and skills. A small icon depicts this sensory tool and is included in the corner of Adam's planner and also on his home page of the VLE; a written reminder on his schedule states: 'Remember, if anxious, use the tangler.'

3   **Social and communication demands in lessons:** if the 'tangle-toy' does not help Adam to feel calm, he is also provided with a visual communication strategy which works well with the visual supports of Structured Teaching. The 'Incredible five point scale' (Buron and Curtis 2003) app is available on Adam's tablet and he has personalised this tool to use five written steps for communicating his level of

Homework: subject and topic		Time allocation	✓
Step 1 **First I need to...**	Research the topic	20 minutes	
Step 2 **...then**	Select a mind-map template	5 minutes	
Step 3 **...then**	Put first idea onto the mind-map template	5 minutes	
Step 4 **Finally**	Add ideas and show how they connect using colour coded branches	15 minutes	
Keep the finished mind-map to use in the next lesson.			
When I have finished my homework I may choose a leisure activity.			

Figure 9.10 Visual template to structure ideas for homework.

anxiety (see Figure 9.11). The use of traffic lights helps Adam to express how he is feeling and he is able to select how he is feeling to display in a corner of the screen on his tablet – this alerts adults and reduces pressure on Adam by not requiring him to verbally communicate how he is feeling. As with the 'tangler' strategy, Adam has a written reminder to use the app included in his planner (see Figure 9.12).

		How do I feel?	What I can do
5 (red)	Panic stations!	I am panicking, I am losing control, I might start to use bad language	Show number 5 (red) on tablet Place red card on desk and go to safe place (inclusion unit)
4 (amber/red)	I am very anxious	I am sweating a little I am getting a headache I am confused	Show number 4 (amber/red) on tablet Request break
3 (amber)	I am worried	I am still anxious, I am worried and do not know what to do and can't hear instructions	Show number 3 amber on tablet Breathe, squeeze stress ball
2 (green/amber)	I getting a little anxious	I am confused ????	Breathe in and out slowly Show number 2 anxious on tablet Ask TA for help
1 (green) ☺	I feel good	Relaxed and calm	Show number 1 green and smiley face on tablet

Figure 9.11 Five-point anxiety scale.

4   **Less structured break times:** to build Adam's self-confidence, he is appointed as a break time buddy to a younger student (Billy) who also has Asperger Syndrome and dyslexia. Adam is provided with 'being a buddy' rules and spends two break times each week with Billy. One break time is spent playing chess, an interest they share, and during the other break time, Adam listens to Billy read. For this to work, both boys need clear visual rules and supports.

Figure 9.11 illustrates Adam's 'menu' of strategies which combines: visual structure and supports which include a visual mind-mapping app; a sensory strategy, anxiety scale and communication tool; a confidence-building role as a buddy.

Menu of anxiety busting tips for feeling confident

Remember: check my schedule and read my instructions. I can use my planner and/or my tablet.

Homework: use the homework template & use my mind-map to plan my work

Anxiety in lessons: use my tangler.

If I am still anxious, use my anxiety scale

Building confidence: be a buddy for Billy – break 1 play chess, break 2 listen to Billy read.

Figure 9.12 Reminder of strategies to reduce anxiety.

This combination of strategies works well for Adam by providing strategies to support his academic work and also, and perhaps more importantly, help him to use strategies to manage his anxieties and build his self-confidence. Adam's 'menu' exemplifies the blending of strategies where Structured Teaching provides a framework within which varied strategies may be selected by Adam, staff and parents.

Conclusion

It is widely recognised that no single approach will meet the learning needs of an individual with ASD. For example, Jones *et al.* (2008) explain:

> Given the diversity within the spectrum and between individuals, there is no single educational intervention that is useful for all children on the autism spectrum, and there is no single intervention that would on its own be sufficient to meet all the needs of a particular child on the autism spectrum.
>
> (p. 15)

Classroom practices for learners with ASD are, not surprisingly, eclectic; teachers in specialist and mainstream settings select different approaches for different learners, according to needs. Structured Teaching provides a framework for this eclectic practice. This framework is flexible and responsive to individual needs and strengths and provides the meaningful structure for learners with ASD that enhances their learning and hence their access to the curriculum. Within this structured framework, however, other approaches can be combined according to individual needs and priorities so Structured Teaching provides a solid foundation that helps everyone and allows for the individualised adjustments that the unique learning needs of each person with ASD will benefit from.

Bibliography

American Psychiatric Association (2013) *Diagnostic and Statistical Manual of Mental Disorders*, 5th edn (*DSM-5*). Washington, DC: American Psychiatric Association.

Bondy, A.S. and Frost, L.A. (1994) 'The Picture Exchange System', *Focus on Autistic Behaviour* 9(3), 1–19.

Buron, K.D. and Curtis, M. (2003) *The Incredible 5-Point Scale*. Overland Park, KS: Autism Asperger Publishing Co.

Charman, T., Pellicano, L., Peacey, L., Peacey, N., Forward, K. and Dockrell, J. (2011) *What is Good Practice in Autism Education?* London: AET.

Cumine, V., Dunlop, J. and Stevenson, G. (2010) *Asperger Syndrome: A Practical Guide for Teachers*. Oxford: Routledge.

Department for Education (2013) *National Curriculum in England: Framework for Key Stage 1 to 4*. London: DfE.

DfES (2002) *ASD – Guidance from the Autism Working Group*. London: DfES.

Frith, U. (1989) *Autism: Explaining the Enigma*. Oxford: Blackwell.

Grandin, T. (1995) *Thinking in Pictures and Other Reports from my Life with Autism*. New York: Doubleday.

Gray, C. (2010) *The New Social Story Book*. Arlington: Future Horizons.

Greenspan, S. and Wieder, S. (2006) *Engaging Autism: Using the Floortime Approach to Help Children Relate, Communicate and Think*. Cambridge, MA: DaCapo Press.

Hewett, D., Firth, G., Barber, M. and Harrison, T. (2011) *The Intensive Interaction Handbook*. London: Sage.

Howley, M. and Rose, R. (2003) 'Facilitating Group Work for Pupils with Autistic Spectrum Disorders by Combining Jigsawing and Structured Teaching', *Good Autism Practice* 4(1), 20–25.

International Baccalaureate [online] *Access and Advancement*. Available at: www.ibo.org/accessandadvancement/ (accessed 3 April 2014).

International Primary Curriculum [online] *IPC Learning Goals*. Available at: www.greatlearning.com/ipc/the-ipc/ipc-learning-goals (accessed 3 April 2014).

Jones, G., English, A., Guldberg, K., Jordan, R., Richardson, P. and Waltz, M. (2008) *Education Provision for Children and Young People on the Autism Spectrum Living in England: A Review of Current Practice, Issues and Challenges*. London: Autism Education Trust.

Jordan, R. (1999) *Autistic Spectrum Disorders: An Introductory Handbook for Practitioners*. London: David Fulton.

Jordan, R. (2005) 'Autistic Spectrum Disorders'. In Lewis, A. and Norwich, B. (eds) *Special Teaching for Special Children*. Maidenhead: Open University Press/McGraw-Hill, pp. 110–22.

Mesibov, G.B., Adams, L.W. and Klinger, L.G. (1997) *Autism: Understanding the Disorder*. New York: Plenum Press.

Mesibov, G.B., Shea, V. and Schopler, E. (2005) *The TEACCH Approach to Autism Spectrum Disorders*. New York: Springer.

Prizant, B., Wetherby, A., Rubin, E., Laurent, A. and Rydell, P. (2005a) *The SCERTS Model: A Comprehensive Educational Approach for Children with Autism Spectrum Disorders: Program Planning and Intervention Volume 1 Assessment.*

Prizant, B., Wetherby, A., Rubin, E., Laurent, A. and Rydell, P. (2005b) *The SCERTS Model: A Comprehensive Educational Approach for Children with Autism Spectrum Disorders: Program Planning and Intervention Volume 2 Intervention.*

Rogers, S. and Dawson, G. (2010) *Early Start Denver Model for Young Children with Autism: Promoting Language, Learning & Engagement.* New York: Guilford.

Rose, R. and Howley, M. (2007) *Practical Guide to Special Educational Needs in Inclusive Primary Classrooms.* London: Sage.

Sainsbury, C. (2000) *Martian in the Playground.* Bristol: Lucky Duck.

Schopler, E., Mesibov, G. and Hearsey, K. (1995) 'Structured Teaching in the TEACCH System'. In Schopler, E. and Mesibov, G. (eds) *Learning and Cognition in Autism.* New York: Plenum, pp. 243–268.

Wing, L. and Gould, J. (1979) 'Severe Impairments of Social Interaction and Associated Abnormalities in Children: Epidemiology and Classification', *Journal of Autism and Childhood Schizophrenia* 9, 11–29.

Wolff, S. (1998) 'Schizoid Personality in Childhood: The Links with Asperger Syndrome, Schizophrenia Spectrum Disorders and Elective Mutism'. In Schopler, E., Mesibov, G.B. and Kunce, L.J. (eds) *Asperger Syndrome or High-functioning Autism?* New York: Plenum Press, pp. 123–142.

World Health Organisation (WHO) (1992) *The ICD-10 Classification of Mental and Behavioural Disorders: Diagnostic Criteria for Research.* Geneva: WHO.

Index

Page numbers in *italics* denote tables, those in **bold** denote figures.